W9-BME-156

Mastery of Your Anxiety and Panic

DAVID H. BARLOW Ph.D

MICHELLE G. CRASKE Ph.D

Center for Stress and Anxiety Disorders
UNIVERSITY at ALBANY
STATE UNIVERSITY OF NEW YORK

Drs. Barlow and Craske have written an outstanding teaching module to be used by patients who suffer from panic, agoraphobia and related anxiety states. The manual will be an invaluable addition to standard clinical treatment and a godsend to patients who live in areas where such treatment is not available.

M. Katherine Shear, M.D.
Director, Anxiety Disorders Clinic
Payne Whitney Clinic
Cornell University Medical College

This method of treating panic attacks is clearly the best conceived and most useful approach yet devised. Dr. Barlow and Dr. Craske have made an important and effective advance in anxiety treatment.

Jack M. Gorman, M.D.
Chief, Department of Clinical Psychobiology
New York State Psychiatric Institute and
College of Physicians and Surgeons,
Columbia University

Drs. Barlow and Craske's manual is a great step forward in helping patients to gain control over panic attacks. It is simply the best of its kind.

Scott Woods, M.D.
Director, Anxiety Disorders Clinic
Yale University Medical School

ABOUT THE AUTHORS

DAVID H. BARLOW

MICHELLE G. CRASKE

DAVID H. BARLOW received his Ph.D. from the University of Vermont in 1969 and has published over 150 articles and chapters and nine books, mostly in the areas of anxiety disorders, sexual problems, and clinical research methodology. Recent books include: Barlow, D.H. (1985), Clinical Handbook of Psychological Disorders: A Step-by-Step Treatment Manual, New York: Guilford Press; Barlow, D.H. & Cerny, J.A. (1988), Psychological Treatment of Panic, New York: Guilford Press; and his latest book, Barlow, D.H. (1988), Anxiety and its Disorders: The Nature and Treatment of Anxiety and Panic, New York: Guilford Press.

He was formerly Professor of Psychiatry and Psychology at Brown University. Currently, he is Professor in the Department of Psychology at the State University of New York at Albany, Co-Director of the Center for Stress and Anxiety Disorders and Director of the Phobia and Anxiety Disorders Clinic. He has been a consultant to the National Institute of Mental Health (NIMH) and the National Institutes of Health since 1973 and was recently awarded a merit award from the NIMH for "...research competence and productivity that are distinctly superior...". The major objective of his work for the last ten years has been the development of new treatments for anxiety disorders.

MICHELLE G. CRASKE received her Ph.D. from the University of British Columbia in 1985 and has published many articles and chapters in the area of anxiety disorders. Currently, she is an Adjunct Assistant Professor in the Department of Psychology at the State University of New York at Albany, in addition to her position as Senior Research Scientist and Associate Director of the Phobia and Anxiety Disorders Clinic within the Center for Stress and Anxiety Disorders at the State University of New York at Albany. Her research has focused upon the development of specific treatments for anxiety, panic and avoidance restrictions, and upon variables of etiological and maintaining significance for patterns of fear and avoidance. She is currently a member of the DSM-IV Anxiety Disorders Workgroup Subcommittee for revision of the diagnostic criteria surrounding Panic Disorder.

ACKNOWLEDGEMENTS

We wish to acknowledge with deep appreciation the contribution of all present and former students and staff of the Center for Stress and Anxiety Disorders to the development of this treatment program. In particular, Jerry Cerny, Ph.D. and Janet Klosko, Ph.D. made invaluable contributions to our earlier version of the protocol. Finally, Ron Rapee, Ph.D. made a substantial contribution to the current program and should be considered one of the originators.

We would also like to acknowledge that two of "The Far Side" cartoons by Gary Larson are reprinted by permission of Chronicle Features, San Francisco, California. Permission was also granted to reprint several of Gary Larson's cartoons by the Universal Press Syndicate, all rights reserved.

TABLE OF CONTENTS

CHAPTER 4

CHAPTER 5

CHAPTER 6

CHAPTER 7

Refinement of Physical Response Control Techniques and an
Introduction to Self-Statement Analysis

CHAPTER 8

Continuation of Self-Statement Analysis: Manipulating Your Own Mind

CHAPTER 9

The Unexpected Becomes Predictable

CHAPTER 10

CHAPTER 11

CHAPTER 12

CHAPTER 13

CHAPTER 14

CHAPTER 15

ANSWERS FOR SELF-ASSESSMENT QUESTIONS

MASTERY OF YOUR ANXIETY AND PANIC WITHOUT DRUGS

CHAPTER 1

<u>Controlled By or Control Over Your Emotions</u>

<u>What is Panic and Anxiety: Is this Program Right for You?</u>

Do you feel at the mercy of your own emotions? Do you experience repeated surges of emotion that make you think you're sick, dying, or losing your mind? When these episodes occur, does your heart feel like it's going to burst out of your chest? Do you feel dizzy, faint, trembly, sweaty, short of breath, and scared to death? Many people who have these kinds of experiences feel as if they are continually on guard for scary feelings, and, therefore, are constantly on edge, even when doing things that they used to enjoy or find relaxing. These scary feelings may interfere with what they do in their daily lives. Often they avoid activities that bring on those feelings, such as drinking coffee. When they get into a car or go into a crowded store, they anticipate the scary feelings and worry about how they might tolerate them or how they can escape if they have to. Sometimes these feelings of terror seem to come from out of the blue when they are least expected, such as while at home relaxing. People with these problems often pay very close attention to different aspects of their bodily functioning (such as their breathing or their blood pressure) because any slight irregularity may suggest that those scary feelings are coming on again. Most people think that the feelings are going to cause them to die, faint, collapse, go crazy or be very embarrassed.

Does this come close to describing you? If so, chances are you're experiencing panic attacks and associated severe anxiety. Of course, there are many individual differences in the way in which panic and anxiety are experienced and their effects on daily life. If you experience something like what was described above, then it is likely that the program in this manual will be helpful for you, as it has been for many people who have come to our clinic, including an individual we shall call Steve.

Steve was a 35 year old, single, sales manager who suffered episodes of dizziness, blurred vision, heart palpitations and loss of concentration. The first episode occurred at work, in the presence of his fellow workers, and began with feelings of weakness, nausea, and dizziness. He thought he was going to faint and asked one of his colleagues to call a doctor. It seemed to him at the time that he could be suffering a stroke. His father had recently died of a heart attack. In addition, Steve was also dealing with a lot of stress at work.

Several months before that first episode, Steve had had times when he was nervous and his writing had become shaky, but apart from that, he had never experienced anything like this before. After a thorough physical exam, his doctor told him that it was stress and anxiety and referred him to our Anxiety Disorders Clinic. By the time he arrived at our clinic, the panic episodes were occurring mostly at work, when driving, in restaurants, and at home. They were often unexpected, particularly the times that he woke from a sound sleep in a state of panic. In general, between the times that he experienced the episodes of panic, he reported a lot of tension and anxiety. He reported symptoms such as a general state of jumpiness, restlessness, inability to relax, difficulty sleeping, difficulty concentrating, muscle twitching, pressure feelings around his chest, and a loss of confidence in himself. Since his third panic attack, he had begun to avoid being alone whenever possible because he was afraid that if he panicked his life could be in real danger. He also avoided situations such as stores, malls, crowds, theaters, and waiting in lines because he was afraid of being trapped and embarrassed if he panicked. When he did experience an attack, he would typically escape from the situation or ask for help. He carried with him a bible, as well as gum and cigarettes wherever he went since glancing at the bible or chewing gum or smoking cigarettes would make him feel more comfortable and better able to cope.

Susan was another person who benefited greatly from the kind of program described in this manual. She was 24 years old and single, and reported repeated attacks of dizziness, breathlessness, palpitations, chest pain, blurred vision, a lump in her throat, and a feeling of unreality, all of which was accompanied by a feeling of impending doom. That is, she was afraid that she was going to have a heart attack or just lose control. The problem began around two years earlier following one of her first experiences with marijuana. While at a party she had smoked some of the drug and within a short while began to feel very unreal and dizzy. Susan thought she was very ill and was afraid that she was no longer in control. She asked one of her friends to take her to the Emergency Room. She had gone back to the Emergency Room on at least two other occasions. The attacks had varied over the years in both intensity and frequency. At one point, she had no attacks for three months. Between attacks, Susan experienced a marked fear of the next possible attack. She felt somewhat uneasy in situations where she thought she would be trapped if an attack occurred but did not actually avoid many different places. She took alprazolam (Xanax) to help her cope with her panics.

If you have experienced these kind of feelings in the past and are currently not fearful, but would like to have some information that might be helpful in the event of a return of your fear, this manual should be worthwhile. However, the program described in this manual is designed primarily for those who are currently experiencing panic attacks or who are currently anxious or worried about panicking or about other related bodily sensations.

Do You Have Panic Disorder or Agoraphobia?

The diagnostic and classification system in use within the United States and many other countries (referred to as the Diagnostic and Statistical Manual, 3rd edition Revised [DSM-III-R], published by the American Psychiatric Association) identifies the problem which this manual addresses as Panic Disorder with or without Agoraphobia. In this disorder, the central component is one or more episodes of intense fear or discomfort such as those experienced by Steve and Susan. At least one of these episodes must be unexpected and not caused by situations in which an individual is the focus of other people's attention, such as when giving a speech at a meeting. These episodes are accompanied by a variety of physical symptoms such as those presented in Table 1:1. Note that fears of going crazy, dying or losing control also accompany these attacks.

These panic attacks are sometimes accompanied by avoidance of situations, places, or activities. Typically the avoided places or situations are those from which escape might be difficult or in which help might be unavailable in the event of a panic attack. A common situation is a large, crowded shopping mall where it might be hard to find the exit and difficult to get through all of the

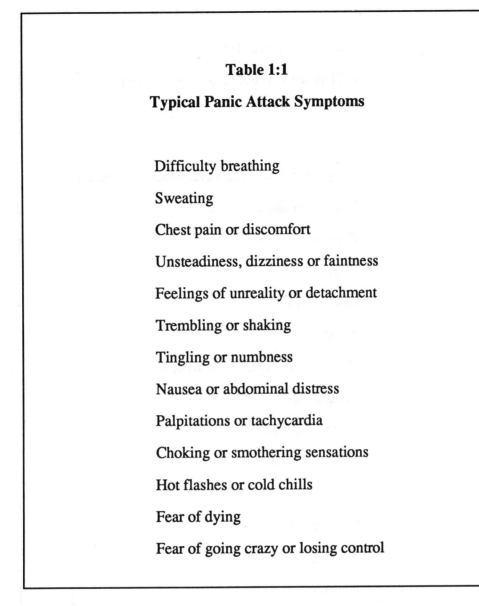

Table 1:1

Typical Panic Attack Symptoms

Difficulty breathing

Sweating

Chest pain or discomfort

Unsteadiness, dizziness or faintness

Feelings of unreality or detachment

Trembling or shaking

Tingling or numbness

Nausea or abdominal distress

Palpitations or tachycardia

Choking or smothering sensations

Hot flashes or cold chills

Fear of dying

Fear of going crazy or losing control

people, in the event one felt they had to leave suddenly because of a panic attack. Even worse would be passing out in front of all those people. Avoiding places or situations because of fear or panic, when no real danger exists, is called a phobia. Avoiding places or situations from which escape might be difficult or help unavailable in the event of a panic attack is called agoraphobia. This is fitting since agora was the ancient Greek marketplace, or, the original shopping mall. However, places and situations typically avoided by people with agoraphobic avoidance behavior are not limited to shopping malls. A partial list is found in Table 1:2.

To meet the diagnostic criteria for panic disorder, it must also be established that these episodes of panic are not the direct result of a physical problem such as hyperthyroidism or excessive amphetamine or caffeine use (which would entail drinking 10 or more cups of coffee per day). That does not mean that physical problems may not be present. For example, it is certainly possible to have both mitral valve prolapse and panic disorder, and control of the mitral valve prolapse symptoms may not necessarily eliminate the panic disorder. Nevertheless, we recommend to our patients who have

---

Table 1:2

Typical Situations Avoided by Agoraphobics

Driving

Public transport - subways, buses, planes, taxis

Waiting in lines

Crowds

Stores

Restaurants

Theaters

Going a long distance from home

Long walks

Wide, open spaces

Closed in spaces

Boats

Staying at home alone

Auditoriums

Elevators

Escalators

---

not had a medical check up in the past year to have a full medical examination to check for possible physical causes of some panic and anxiety symptoms and to identify important physical factors to take into account during the course of the treatment program.

How Common is this Problem?

Panic attacks and agoraphobia are very common. For example, the prevalence rate of agoraphobia is estimated to be 3 to 6 percent of the general population. This means that in the United States alone 7 to 12 million people suffer from agoraphobia. In combination with other phobic and anxiety disorders, the percentage of the general population increases to approximately 10 to 12%.

This represents a larger proportion of the general population than those afflicted with alcohol or drug abuse problems and makes anxiety disorders the number one mental health problem in the United States. More attention has been devoted to the problem of panic and agoraphobia recently, because we now know more about the problem and we can recognize it more easily when people come in to emergency rooms or doctors' offices.

In addition to all of the people mentioned above who have panic disorder and agoraphobia, the experience of a single panic attack in the general population is even more common. For example, over 30% of the population has experienced some sort of panic attack during the past year, often in response to a very stressful situation such as just before an exam or giving a speech. Even with restriction of the definition to panics that seem to occur out of the blue and are not tied to a particularly stressful situation (such as exams), these experiences are reported by as many as 9 to 14% of the population during the past year. But, as we have seen above, far fewer people develop a severe problem that they have to do something about. This implies that most people who have the experience of panic have ways of coping successfully with their panic attacks. We will discuss this further when we talk about ways to manage your own anxiety and panic.

The experience of panic and avoidance seems to occur across all kinds of people: across all levels of socioeconomic status, professions and types of persons. It is also present in many different cultures although it may be labeled and understood differently. Panic is a very common phenomenon that is present in all the different kinds of anxiety problems, but the kind of panic attacks for which this program is designed are the attacks which perpetuate themselves and become the very thing that is dreaded.

How Are You Coping With Your Panic Attacks Now?

We already mentioned above a very common way of coping with panic attacks; that is, to avoid situations where they might occur. It is such a common method of coping that this phobic avoidance behavior has its own label: agoraphobia. But there are many other methods of coping with panic that people try at one time or another. Many of these methods help people get through a panic attack but do nothing to prevent future attacks. Furthermore, while some of the methods are not harmful, other methods of coping can be extremely dangerous.

We shall describe the different methods of coping.

Avoidance

We have already mentioned agoraphobic avoidance above, but there are many other types of avoidance that are more subtle which are nevertheless connected to panic attacks. For example:

Do you avoid drinking coffee?
Do you avoid drinking alcohol?
Do you avoid medication of any kind even if your doctor prescribes it?
Do you avoid exercise?
Do you avoid becoming very angry?

Do you avoid sexual relations?

Do you avoid watching very emotional movies such as horror movies or even
very sad movies?

Do you avoid being outside in very hot or very cold conditions?

Do you hate being startled or frightened?

Do you avoid being away from medical help?

Do you avoid standing and walking without structural support such as a rail or a wall?

If so, these forms of avoidance may well be connected to your panic attacks and should disappear when you successfully complete this program.

Distraction

Many people attempt to "get through" situations in which they are afraid of having panic attacks by distracting themselves. There is no limit to the ingenuity of methods that have been used as means of distraction. For example, if you feel yourself becoming anxious or panicky, do you:

Play loud music?

Carry around something to read such as the Bible, or some helpful coping
statements, and read them as intensely as you can?

Pinch yourself?

Snap a rubberband on your wrist?

Breath into a paper bag?

Place cold wet towels on your face?

Tell somebody who is with you to talk to you about something - anything?

Try to imagine yourself somewhere else?

Play counting games?

Think about caring for the persons with you - such as your children?

If you have tried many of these tricks (or if you are still using them), chances are they have helped you get through a panic attack in the past and may well help you in the future. However, these tricks often become strong habits in themselves to the extent that many people come to depend on them. Therefore, if you forget your reading material or your rubberband, you may have to go all the way back to your house to get it, or just not go where you had planned to go because you don't have your distractor. In the long run, these strategies, while not harmful, are not helpful since they do not change the core element of panic attacks or your anxiety over the future occurrence of your attacks.

Superstitious Coping Methods

Many people carry around bottles of minor tranquilizers to take if they feel an anxiety or panic attack coming on. If this is done under the supervision of your physician, it is perfectly alright, since he or she will make sure you are not abusing these drugs. However, when not done under supervision, this is a dangerous practice. Less dangerous is a habit many other people have fallen into. They carry around empty bottles of pills in their purse or pocket. These people realize that there is nothing in the bottles that would help them if they have a panic attack. Nevertheless, they feel "better" and "safer" just having that bottle. This is a good example of superstitious behavior that people acquire to protect them from the ravages of out of control emotions (or other real or imagined dangers). Recently, we compiled a list of these safety objects or talismen used by some of our patients. This list is presented below.

List of Safety Signals

Medication
Food or Drink
Smelling Salts or Antacid
Paper Bags
Religious Symbols
Objects such as Flashlights, Money, CB Radios, Cameras, Bags & Bracelets
Reading Material
Cigarettes
Alcohol
Relaxation Tapes, Coping Statements, Therapist's Phone Number
Pets

Obviously, some of these items might also be used as methods of distraction. The difference between distractions and safety signals lies in the intent. Is the object carried because just having it on hand makes the person feel safer, or because it is used to keep the person's mind off their feelings of fear and anxiety?

Drugs and Alcohol

However, it is possible that you use a far more dangerous drug to cope with your panic attacks - alcohol. We now know that many men (more men than women) take a drink to get through their next business meeting or other place or situation where they might have a panic attack. In fact, we now have startling statistics which tell us that from one-third to one-half of those with alcohol problems began down the long road to alcohol addiction by "self-medicating" anxiety or panic. Using alcohol to cope with your panics and anxiety is extremely dangerous. This is because while alcohol works for a little while, it is likely you will become dependent on the alcohol and require more and more of it. As you drink more and more, the anxiety reducing properties of the alcohol become less and less. In fact, your anxiety and depression will increase, putting you in an ever deepening downward spiral of addiction. If you drink to control your anxiety, make every effort to stop as soon as possible: ask your doctor or mental health professional for help.

Other Disorders

Panic attacks occur not only occur in all types of anxiety disorders but are also often present in mood disorders, such as depression. If you experience panic within the context of feelings of sadness, hopelessness, loss of interest, and loss of energy, then consult with your mental health professional to learn if an alternative form of treatment is more appropriate than this manual.

What Causes Panic and Anxiety?

This is a very difficult question and we don't know all the answers just yet. Furthermore, we won't be spending a great deal of time on this subject at this point since you will learn more about it in some of the following chapters as you begin to master your anxiety and panic. But it is important to say several things about the causes of panic and anxiety.

First, the research does not suggest that panic attacks are due to a disease or a biological dysfunction. Of course, there are the relatively rare examples mentioned above where a physical condition does result in symptoms that resemble a panic attack, as would be the case with hyperthyroidism or a tumor on the adrenal gland. However, common panic attacks as described above, suffered daily by millions of individuals, do not seem to be due to biological dysfunction. But, biological processes are heavily implicated in panic as we will describe in more detail below.

Similarly, our research shows that cognitive processes or what you are thinking in and of itself does not cause panic. Once again, cognitive processes or thoughts are heavily involved in panic but are not the sole cause. We will also describe the involvement of your thoughts in panic attacks in subsequent chapters.

Panic attacks do seem to be a surge of emotion or fear which by itself is a perfectly normal bodily response. What makes it abnormal is that it occurs at the wrong time; that is, when there is no real reason to be emotional or afraid. Again, the response itself seems perfectly normal and natural and would be the same kind of reaction you would have if real danger (such as facing a gunman) was present. It is also perfectly normal and natural to become anxious about having another panic attack and to be on guard for it to occur. Anxiety such as this will occur anytime we feel that something is potentially dangerous or out of control.

Finally, panic attacks, particularly the first panic attack, seem to occur unexpectedly during a time when people feel generally uptight or under a great deal of stress. If someone close to you has died, if you are under considerable pressure at work or at home, if you are having difficulties in your marriage or with your children, then you are more likely to have a panic attack, if panic is a reaction to which you are susceptible. Some people don't have panic attacks when they're emotional or under stress, but rather have other types of reactions such as headaches, high blood pressure or ulcers. However, if you are susceptible to experiencing panic, then even happy occasions might result in panic attacks if they involve major changes in your life. Stress can be both positive and negative. For example, moving to a new home, even if the home is bigger and nicer, having a baby or getting married all can set the occasion for panic attacks in susceptible individuals. We will say more about the causes of panic, anxiety and stress and how to control these reactions in the chapters to follow[1].

[1]For a complete account of all of the most recent research on the nature and causes of anxiety and panic you may wish to read Anxiety and Its Disorders: The Nature and Treatment of Anxiety and Panic by David H. Barlow, published in 1988, by Guilford Press, 72 Spring Street, New York, New York 10012.

<u>Do You Fit This Program</u>?

The following table will help you to determine whether you are a suitable candidate for this particular program.

Have you had:

(1)   Repeated episodes of extreme fear (panic) or a lot of anxious anticipation of experiencing another panic attack.

(2)   At least some of the episodes are accompanied by physical sensations and thoughts such as:

> difficulty breathing
> choking or smothering sensations
> heart palpitations or tachycardia
> chest pain or discomfort
> trembling or shaking
> sweating
> dizziness, unsteadiness or faintness
> hot or cold flashes
> nausea or abdominal distress
> feelings of unreality, detachment
> numbness or tingling
> fears of dying, going crazy or losing control

(3)   At least one of the panic episodes was unexpected or came out of the blue.

(4)   A general state of anxiety, vigilance, or being on edge for the next panic or scary bodily sensation.

(5)   A range from none to severe levels of avoidance of different activities and situations in which panic is expected or feared to occur.

(6)   The major problem revolves around the experience of panic, instead of fear of other specific objects, fear of social evaluation, contamination or self doubt, or chronic worrying about future events.

(7)   The panics are not directly attributable to physical (organic) causes.

<u>Alternate Treatments</u>

The kind of contact you have had with other mental health professionals in the past and the use of different drugs does not mean that you are not appropriate for this particular program. We have used this program time and time again with people who have been through many different forms of treatment. However, some consideration must be given to other kinds of treatment that may be ongoing with your participation in this program. We recommend that if you undertake this program, it should <u>not</u> be in conjunction with other forms of psychotherapy that are also focused specifically on the treatment of panic. As with all treatments or programs that are focused on the same problem, messages can become mixed and confused. For that reason, we find it much more effective to do only one at a time. However, if a concurrent psychotherapy program is very general in its orientation or is focused on a very different problem area, then there is no reason why the two cannot be done at the same time.

If you are involved in another program right now that is specifically focused upon the treatment of panic, we recommend that you pursue that program until you are sure that either it is effective (in which case no more treatment is needed) or it is ineffective (in which case this program can be tried). As you will soon see, this program has been found to be very effective for many people, but that does not mean that other programs will necessarily be less effective for you and should not be given a fair trial. Different forms of therapy are more or less effective for different people. You must make this decision if you are involved in a concurrent panic treatment program. Of course, ideally you would be working on this program together with your doctor or mental health professional who may have handed you this manual.

Are You Taking Drugs for Your Anxiety?

If you currently use drugs for the control of anxiety and panic, this program will still be appropriate. For some people, drugs are only mildly to moderately effective or not effective at all. For others, drugs are effective initially but relapse occurs when the drug is stopped. Combining drug treatment with this program has been successful. If you have an interest in stopping the drugs you are currently taking, then we suggest some important points to consider later in the manual that can be combined with direct medical supervision of the withdrawal process after completing this program. It is definitely not wise to stop taking medication on your own.

What Benefits Will You Receive From This Program

What should you expect to get out of this program? This information is important in your evaluation of whether to become involved. From research studies conducted at our Center for Stress and Anxiety Disorders designed to evaluate the effectiveness of our panic-treatment program, it seems that this treatment is very successful. The percentage of people who report that they are free of panic at the completion of a program similar to this one is from 80-90%. What is more exciting is that these results seem to maintain over long periods of time — up to 24 months after treatment, which is the longest period we have examined. One of the reasons for this maintenance effect is that the treatment is essentially a learning program. When something is learned, it becomes a natural part of one's reactions and, therefore, you carry with you everything you have learned even after the formal program has been completed. Obviously, there is never a guarantee that this treatment will be the one for you or that you may never panic again, but from the success rates it would seem that this program is worth trying.

If you avoid a number of situations, we know that treatment programs focused on the avoidance per se produce significant improvements in 60 to 80% of our patients. Again, this is maintained, and often improves further, up to two years after treatment completion. In combination with techniques for the treatment of panic, it is likely that this percentage of success will increase even more. We also know that including someone from your own family or circle of friends may help you to implement

CHAPTER 2

Learning About Your Reactions

Why Should You Learn to Be An Observer?

A big part of the feeling of loss of control stems from being carried along by habitual emotional responses without ever successfully stepping back outside of the emotional cycle and observing what is going on. To begin to change, one must first be very aware of what occurs naturally and what needs to be changed. You must become a behavioral scientist rather than a victim in the jungle of your emotions awaiting the next attack. Observation of your reactions means carefully monitoring when the emotion occurs, under what circumstances it occurs (which will start to inform you about the triggers) and the exact sequence of events (which will start to inform you about how the emotional cycle is escalated). Then you will be in a position to make more valid judgments about what is going on, to institute the most appropriate methods of change and to evaluate the effectiveness of your methods.

Tailoring the program to your needs is based very much on how well a particular strategy works for you. That evaluation is based on information gathered from observational records. It has been shown over and over again that global descriptions of one's emotional reaction some time after the emotional event has occurred is much less accurate than giving an on the spot account of what is felt and what has happened. This is because our memories are colored by our mood, so that if you are generally anxious you will remember events as being more fearful than they were at the time. Similarly, feeling depressed results in recalling more negative, sad events than positive ones. The biasing effect of mood upon memory is part of the reason why fear continues on in a vicious cycle. We will talk more about this below. Direct observation plays a therapeutic role in breaking that cycle. If you monitor emotional events as they occur, you are much more likely to think about and remember them accurately, which will help to remove some of the biasing memory effects.

By on-the-spot monitoring, you are, therefore, accomplishing several extremely important things:

1. Identifying conditions under which panic attacks are likely to occur. This highlights significant factors for treatment. Does the panic occur primarily when alone or with others, after a stressful day at work or on weekends, etc.?

2. Identifying specific antecedents or triggers for the panic. This is a major task and may be very difficult initially. However, it is a crucial step and enables you to begin to break the perception of being the victim of an unpredictable or uncontrollable event that descends upon you when you least expect it. You may find specific antecedents such as feeling excited by a sports event on TV, feeling hot from the sun, feeling suffocation from a steamy shower, thinking about horrible things that could happen as a result of becoming anxious, facing a particular situation of which you are afraid, or relaxing and having nothing else to do but dwell on your fears. Of course, all of these elements would then be included in the program.

3.   Monitoring allows you to evaluate your progress. The monitoring will be continued throughout the entire program. When feeling anxious, it is easy to dismiss gains and focus instead on still feeling afraid or having difficulties. On-the-spot monitoring will enable you to counter that bias in thinking and to appreciate the gains you make.

Also, for the times when one episode of panic makes you feel like you have failed or fallen back, you can use these monitoring forms to provide a context in which to place that panic and therefore not allow the one incident to overshadow all the progress that you have made.

4.   Monitoring is the first step in gaining control.

What To Monitor

1. Panic attacks should be monitored using the portable record (PANIC ATTACK RECORD) that is on page 2-4 of this manual. Tear it out and make as many copies as you need. This form should be used every time you experience what you consider to be a panic attack — or a sudden rush of fear — over the course of the entire treatment program. Do not wait until the end of the day to complete this form as you will lose accuracy and lose the sense of being an observer. Complete it as soon as possible after you recognize the panic attack. Of course, if you are driving you cannot stop to fill out this record. Or, if you are talking with someone or in the middle of a meeting it is hard to stop and fill out the form. But the monitoring should be done as soon as possible afterwards.

    On the record, note the date, the time of onset and duration of the panic. Also, note with whom it occurred and whether the situation you were in was stressful or not; in other words, a situation that you would expect to make you anxious or fearful. Give a brief description of the stressful event. Identify whether the panic was expected or unexpected at the time that it occurred and the maximum level of fear that you experienced. Rate your level of fear on a 0 to 8 point scale, where 0 = no fear, 2 = mild fear, 4 = moderate fear, 6 = strong fear and 8 = extreme fear. Then, from the list of symptoms, underline the first one noticed, and check off each of the symptoms that were present to a reasonable degree.

    Let's examine the records completed by Jill. Jill is 29 years old, married, and has one child. She began to panic one year ago, when her child was a few months old. Since then, she has been afraid to stay home alone with her baby and so often spends the day at her mother's place, while her husband is at work.

    From her first record, it can be seen that this particular panic occurred at 5:20 p.m. in the afternoon on February 16 and lasted for 15 minutes. She panicked while she was alone (waiting for her husband to return from work) and Jill related the panic to the stressful situation of being alone. It was an expected panic; that is, Jill was not surprised that it happened at this time. Her maximum fear level was six, which is strong. A racing heart was the first symptom she noticed, and during the panic, other symptoms included difficulty breathing, sweating, trembling and shaking, numbness or tingling, feelings of unreality, and a fear of losing control or going crazy. From her second record, it can be seen that her second panic occurred at 3:00 a.m. on February 19, and lasted for five mintues. She panicked while in bed, with her husband, after waking up and spending a few minutes dwelling on her heart rate. It was not a stressful situation, and was an unexpected it panic. Her maximum fear level was 7. She first noticed a racing of her heart rate, and then experienced breathing symptoms, sweating, shaking, and fears of dying.

Table 2:1

PANIC ATTACK RECORD

Date _____ Time began _____ Duration (mins.)_____
Alone _____ Friend _____ Stranger _____ Family_____
Stressful? Yes/No _____
Expected? Yes/No

Maximum Fear: 0——1——2——3—— 4 ——5——6——7——8
                None   Mild   Moderate   Strong   Extreme

Underline first symptom and check all symptoms present:

Difficulty Breathing	_____	Chest Pain/		Fear of Dying	_____
Racing/Pounding Heart	_____	Discomfort	_____	Fear of Losing	
Choking Sensations	_____	Hot/Cold Flashes	_____	Control/Going	
Sweating	_____	Numbness/Tingling	_____	Crazy	_____
Trembling/Shaking	_____	Feelings of			
Nausea/Abdominal		Unreality	_____		
Upset	_____	Unsteadiness/Dizziness/			
		Faintness	_____		

Table 2:2

JILL'S

PANIC ATTACK RECORD

Date <u>February 16</u> Time began <u>5:20 pm</u> Duration (mins.) <u>15</u>
Alone <u>√</u> Friend _____ Stranger _____ Family_____
Stressful? (Yes)/No <u>Waiting for husband to come home from work.</u>
Expected? (Yes)/No

Maximum Fear: 0——1——2——3——4——5—(6)—7——8
　　　　　　　None　　Mild　　Moderate　(Strong)　Extreme

Underline first symptom and check all symptoms present:

Difficulty Breathing	√	Chest Pain/		Fear of Dying	_____
<u>Racing/Pounding Heart</u>	√	Discomfort	_____	Fear of Losing	
Choking Sensations	_____	Hot/Cold Flashes	_____	Control/Going	
Sweating	√	Numbness/Tingling	√	Crazy	√
Trembling/Shaking	√	Feelings of			
Nausea/Abdominal		Unreality	√		
Upset	_____	Unsteadiness/Dizziness/			
		Faintness	_____		

Table 2:3

JILL'S

PANIC ATTACK RECORD

Date <u>February 19</u> Time began <u>3:00 am</u> Duration (mins.) <u>5</u>

Alone _____ Friend _____ Stranger _____ Family __✓__

Stressful? Yes/(No)_____

Expected? Yes/(No)

Maximum Fear: 0——1——2——3——4——5——6——(7)——8
                None   Mild   Moderate   Strong   Extreme

Underline first symptom and check all symptoms present:

Difficulty Breathing	✓	Chest Pain/		Fear of Dying ✓
<u>Racing/Pounding Heart</u>	✓	Discomfort _____		Fear of Losing
Choking Sensations _____		Hot/Cold Flashes _____		Control/Going
Sweating	✓	Numbness/Tingling _____		Crazy _____
Trembling/Shaking	✓	Feelings of		
Nausea/Abdominal		Unreality _____		
Upset _____		Unsteadiness/Dizziness/		
		Faintness _____		

2. It is also important to monitor general levels of anxiety and other moods. The second record (DAILY MOOD RECORD) enables you to record your general levels of anxiety and depression at the end of each day. We find it most helpful to use 0-8 point scales for rating levels of anxiety, levels of depression, and your anticipation or worry about having a panic attack during the day. For all ratings, 8 is the extreme end of the scale: extreme anxiety, extreme depression and extreme anticipation of panic. These ratings are based on how you felt on average over the course of each day. One of these records will last for one week. Again, tear out the form on page 2-8 and make copies for yourself, to last for at least 15 weeks.

By now you will realize that panic attacks are different from just being nervous or anxious, but it is worth repeating this at various points throughout this manual so that you will not confuse the two when using these forms. Panic attacks are the sudden surges of frightening emotion experienced by Steve and Susan as illustrated in the first chapter. Even if one is generally anxious or apprehensive during the day, one might have a sudden surge of panic on top of the anxiety. In fact, these two often go together in this way. Alternatively, a panic attack may come totally out of the blue even when you are asleep and presumably relaxed.

On the other hand, everybody knows what it means to be anxious. Being anxious or nervous or "worrying" quite a bit is something most of us have done. At times, this anxiety may be very intense and severe as it would be when one has to make a speech in front of a group of new and strange people. In fact, if you are like most people, you would probably be very anxious all day long before this speech, but this would be different from the sudden surge of emotion that is a panic attack. Anxiety is best characterized as worrying about something in the future even if the future is only an hour away. Panic, on the other hand, is a surge of emotion associated usually with thoughts of dying or losing control at the present time. In this way, one can be anxious about having a panic attack even though anxiety and panic are closely related emotions. We will talk more about the nature and causes of anxiety and panic in Chapters 3 and 4.

From Jill's Daily Mood Record that is given below, it can be seen that over the course of the week, she had a fluctuating pattern of anxiety, depression, and worry about having a panic attack. On 2/16 and 2/17, Jill was quite worried about having a panic attack; these were the first two days after a weekend spent with her husband. Notice how she was also generally more anxious and depressed on those days compared to other days. Whereas, on the 21st and 22nd (the weekend), she felt less anxious, less depressed and less worried about panicking because her husband was with her the whole time.

Over the course of several weeks, important trends usually become evident, especially in the way these moods fluctuate in relation to the frequency of panic attacks. In your case it will be very important to learn this information to make your treatment as

Table 2:4
<u>DAILY MOOD RECORD</u>

0——1——2——3——4——5——6——7——8
None   Mild   Moderate   Strong   Extreme

Date	Average Anxiety	Average Depression	Average Anticipation/Worry About Panic

Table 2:5

JILL'S

DAILY MOOD RECORD

0——1——2——3——4——5——6——7——8
None　　Mild　　Moderate　　Strong　　Extreme

Date	Average Anxiety	Average Depression	Average Anticipation/Worry About Panic
2/16	5	4	6
2/17	6	4	6
2/18	4	3	5
2/19	3	2	4
2/20	4	4	4
2/21	3	2	2
2/22	2	2	2

3.   It is also important to keep a chart of your improvement based on these monitoring forms. The PROGRESS RECORD is divided into the number of panics per week and the average anxiety per week. Of course, you may also record any other dimensions in which you are particularly interested. This PROGRESS RECORD, like the one shown on page 2-11, will allow you to see objectively how you are doing and to put things into perspective. It is helpful to keep this in a place that is very visible, such as your bathroom mirror or on the refrigerator. Make your own chart by copying the one on page 2-11. Using graph paper would make it easier but it isn't necessary.

4.   We have not talked about the monitoring of your activities and your ability to go places on your own. We shall leave that for later because the initial stages of this program focus on fear and anxiety.

One cannot emphasize enough the importance of this monitoring. It must be done daily to get the full benefit from this program. While at first you may have to push yourself to monitor, it will become easier and even rewarding. It helps to give yourself feedback and it is also beneficial for your mental health professional if you provide this kind of information. These records will be invaluable during the rest of the program so it is definitely worth the effort.

Exercise

Make copies of the monitoring forms (PANIC ATTACK RECORD, DAILY MOOD REC-ORD, and PROGRESS RECORD) and begin to monitor your panics and daily mood levels for a full week. Do not start any other part of the program yet because you are still learning about your reactions. This next week of daily monitoring will be a good test of your motivation.

Self-Assessment

Answer by circling true (T) or false (F). Answers are on page A-1.

1.   Monitoring is very important because it provides a more accurate description of your fear than vague generalities or trying to remember events from the past.   T   F

2.   It is best not to think about how anxious you feel.   T   F

3.   Monitoring of panics is best done at the end of the day.   T   F

4.   Monitoring is essential for the identification of important conditions and specific antecedents that provoke panic.   T   F

5.   Monitoring of anxiety and other moods can wait until the end of the day.   T   F

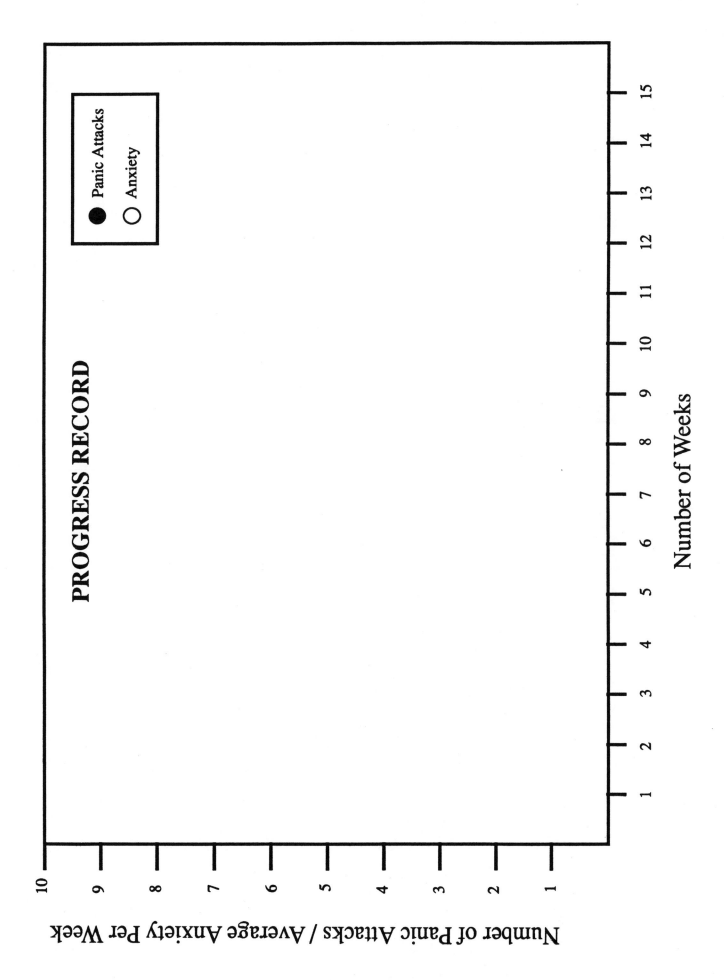

PROGRESS RECORD

Panic Attacks
Anxiety

Number of Weeks

Number of Panic Attacks / Average Anxiety Per Week

CHAPTER 3

Developing a Perspective for Changing Your Reactions

Review Your Records

Did you complete a mood record every day and record panics as they occurred? If not, try to think of ways to improve your compliance with filling in those records as they are essential to the continuation of your program. For example, place the DAILY MOOD RECORD in a very visible place, such as on the refrigerator. Carry your PANIC ATTACK RECORDS with you wherever you go. If you have not done any monitoring, use the following week to monitor before continuing with the program.

Look at the patterns that have emerged from your monitoring. For instance, do the panics typically occur when you are alone or when you are with someone else? Do they occur at a particular time of the day such as in the evening when you are relaxing watching TV? Do they occur more often in difficult or stressful situations than in nonstressful situations? Are the symptoms that you experience the same ones each time or do they vary depending on where the panic occurs? Is the first symptom that is noticed the same each time?

Beginning to identify the patterns is the first step towards identifying factors that relate to your panic. In addition, look for relationships between the PANIC ATTACK RECORD and the DAILY MOOD RECORD. For instance, does panic occur more often when you are feeling generally more anxious or depressed? Does your anxious anticipation of panic increase after you experience panics or before you experience panics? Now that the week of monitoring is over, fill in the data for the first week on the PROGRESS RECORD: number of panics for the week, average daily anxiety rating for the week and whatever else you decide to chart.

Looking for patterns is the first step in learning that the feeling of panic is a <u>reaction</u> - and it is not some automatic response over which you have no control. Calling it a "reaction" implies that there is something you can do to change or learn to react differently. It is this aspect that we will begin to examine shortly. Let's discuss first the nature of anxiety and then in the next lesson we can focus more specifically upon the experience of panic.

What is Anxiety

Anxiety is a natural emotion that is experienced by every single person. Anxiety is part of the experience of being human. Anxiety is not bad in and of itself, and in many cases, is a productive, driving force. Years of research have shown over and over again that having some anxiety enhances performance; that is, you do better at what you're doing whether in the classroom or on the tennis court when anxiety is present up to a certain level. However, anxiety can vary tremendously in severity, from mild uneasiness to extreme distress, and can vary in frequency from occasional distress to seemingly constant unease. It is when anxiety is experienced as very intense or very frequent that it can interfere with an individual's daily life. Hence, the goal of a program such as this is to reduce the frequency and/or intensity of anxiety at times when it is inappropriate but, the goal is not to remove anxiety altogether because that is impossible and, furthermore, undesirable.

Some anxiety is good and is needed for certain levels of performance.

View anxiety as a dimension from none to extreme and place yourself somewhere along that dimension, as you have been doing each day by keeping a DAILY MOOD RECORD. Overall, your anxiety may be at a level that is higher than you want. For that reason, it feels like it is out of your control. Together we will attempt to bring that level down to a point where you feel comfortable overall and can experience some anxiety under certain conditions without feeling as if it is out of your control.

Anxiety is difficult to manage when viewed as a global coherent whole or a "lump". A global approach does not provide clues for controlling anxiety. It is very easy for other people to say "stop being so anxious, just relax" but it is very difficult to use that as a method of control. When anxiety is viewed in terms of its components, however, the task of learning to become less anxious is much easier and, in addition, the understanding of anxiety as a reaction becomes more obvious.

What are the major components of anxiety and panic? The three major components are physiologic, thoughts, and behaviors. Let's explain each one. The physiologic component involves the physical feelings or symptoms such as muscular tension, a rapid pulse, difficulty breathing, a nervous stomach possibly accompanied by diarrhea, frequent or excessive sweating, tremulousness, headaches, stomachaches, and so on. The thoughts or statements that one tells oneself involve the sense of impending doom, thoughts that something terrible is about to happen, a sense of danger, and a great deal of worrying about the present and the future. It is the anticipation of the worst and the apprehension about what is going to happen. It is the feeling that events could proceed uncontrollably or that you may not have control over your reactions. It is a feeling of helplessness in the face of uncertainty. The behavior involves disruption of performance, such as when anxiety reaches a level that interferes with the ability to do a good job, to concentrate, or to give a speech. It involves pacing up and down, restlessness and fidgeting. Behavior also involves escaping from or avoiding certain places or events where anxiety or panic is expected to occur. An example is avoiding talking to certain people because of anxiety about how they may react or how they may evaluate what you say. An example of escaping is leaving a shopping mall as soon as the feelings of anxiety or panic develop.

These three components may vary in their predominance across different people and even vary in their predominance within a person at different times. For some individuals the physiology may be in general more important than the behavior. For example, they may experience a lot of physical tension, headaches, diarrhea, but continue to do different tasks and do them well. In addition, at any given time the physiology may be more important for a certain individual while at another time, thoughts may become more important. At one time, stomach trouble may be the strongest factor, while at another time worrying about feeling embarrassed may be the strongest factor. These differences across time usually depend on the context in which the anxiety is experienced. When at home, stomach upset may become a stronger factor than the concern about being embarrassed whereas the reverse may be the case in a public place. However, all three aspects probably play some role in the experience of anxiety for everyone.

Remember in the last chapter we described anxiety as being generally nervous about

---

Table 3:1

Your Anxiety Components

Major Physical   1._____
Sensations   2._____

Major Thoughts   1._____
                      2._____

Major Behaviors   1._____
                      2._____

---

something bad that might happen as opposed to a panic attack which is a very sudden surge of fear. At present, try to distinguish this feeling of anxiety from the feeling of panic. Think about how you experience general anxiety and record on the lines above the major types of reactions you have. Write down what you typically feel, what you think and what you do when you are anxious on the Anxiety Component Form.

Remember Jill? An example of her major anxiety components is provided. A lot of Jill's general anxiety involves worrying about having enough time during the day to get everything done and also the health of her child and her husband (her thoughts). When anxious, she experiences a lot of muscle tension and headaches (her physical sensations). Also, she often bites her nails and puts things off (her behavior).

Table 3:2

Jill's Anxiety Components

Major Physical   1. Muscle tension and stiffness_____
Sensations   2. Headaches_____

Major Thoughts   1. I won't get everything done on time___
                      2. Maybe my son or husband will get sick

Major Behaviors   1. Nail biting_____
                      2. Procrastination_____

Table 3:3

Your Panic Components

Major Physical Sensations	1._____
	2._____
Major Thoughts	1._____
	2._____
Major Behaviors	1._____
	2._____

It is very important that you recognize that the different components (physiology, thoughts and behaviors) are at least partially independent. That is, they can occur separately at times and yet also interact. For example, you may sometimes feel tense but have no identifiable negative or frightening thoughts. At other times, negative thoughts may directly increase your level of physical tension.

Now do the same for the three response modalities that you experience when you feel panicky. Record what you typically think, what you feel, and what you do when you panic on the Panic Component Form.

Recognize that what you are recording probably differs from what you recorded on the Anxiety Component Form. For example, the thoughts may center on worrying about future events when feeling anxious, in contrast to worrying about immediate danger, such as heart attack or suffocation,

---

Table 3:4

Jill's Panic Components

Major Physical Sensations	1. Racing heart
	2. Dizziness
Major Thoughts	1. I'm losing control
	2. This may never end
Major Behaviors	1. Escape - go home or to mother's place
	2. Don't go to certain places

---

during panic. Similarly, the behaviors are probably different: in anxious states the behavior may involve agitation, fidgeting, and pacing, whereas in panic, it may entail immediate escape and avoidance. The physiologic component in general anxiety may involve muscular tension in contrast to numbness and weakness in panic. Use your PANIC ATTACK RECORDS to help you identify your major physiologic symptoms and thoughts when you experience panic. Jill's list of major responses when panicking is provided as an example. As you can see, her sensations, thoughts and behavior when panicking are very different from the components that characterize her when she feels anxious.

So, there are three major components to anxiety and panic. First, the physiological arousal that is associated with physical sensations or feelings. Second, the thoughts, or put another way, things that you say to yourself (self-statements), beliefs, interpretations, expectations, and imagery. Third, behavior which includes avoidance and escape from frightening situations as well as disruption of performance such as talking to friends, reading, or listening to what others are saying. These three components are frequently closely related. At times, various thoughts may bring about increased physiological arousal which in turn may interfere with your behavior. For example, worrying about getting all of your work completed may result in agitation and restlessness to a level which interferes with your ability to actually concentrate and finish the work. Alternatively, physical sensations may be misinterpreted as signs of panic and result in increased fear. For example, sweating on a hot day may be misinterpreted as a sign of impending panic. Furthermore, struggling to escape a situation may feed into the physical sensations of fear and thoughts of danger.

Therefore, while representing separate components, these systems often interact in ways that serve to create further anxiety and fear or panic. It is the interaction among these response components that results in a spiral into extreme anxiety and fear. Try to think about a recent anxiety episode and the sequence of events that led up to the high point of the anxiety. Remember, anxiety is separate from panic. What was the first thing that happened: was it physical tension, was it a thought that something bad was about to happen, or was it procrastination or performance disruption. Try to describe to yourself the sequence of events. For example, Jill experienced a high level of anxiety on a Friday afternoon when she was sitting at her mother's house. Her child was at a friend's place for a birthday party and her husband was at work. After she took her son to the birthday party, she began to feel somewhat anxious because she was concerned about something - anything - happening to him while she was not there to protect him. At her mother's place, she watched a TV newscast about some children who had been kidnapped. Her immediate reaction was to think more about the safety of her own child. This spiralled into worrying about the safety of her husband. She began to pace and feel agitated and worry more and more about the safety of her family, with images of being left on her own and not being able to cope. This, in turn, produced further agitation, restlessness, sweating and a headache. She tried to concentrate on reading but kept going back to the worries in her mind. Here, the sequence of events was a misinterpretation or a self-statement that something bad was going to happen, followed by physiological arousal, followed by further worry, followed by further arousal and interference with performance (anxiety interfered with her ability to read). Try to perform the same kind of analysis for a recent anxiety episode that you have experienced. Look at it objectively as an observer rather than simply stating that you felt anxious. Remember, it is not only a questioning of the original cause of the anxiety, but the sequence through which the anxiety develops. Why does anxiety become more severe or more enduring at any given time? Why didn't Jill's anxiety stop right after she had the concern about the safety of her son? It was because she added to it further agitation, arousal and further concern. Alternatively, she could have interrupted the anxiety spiral early on by reassuring herself in some ways we'll talk about below.

Now do the same for recent panic attacks. What was the first thing that happened, what followed and how did the fear spiral? Some examples, from Jill's analyses of panic-sequences are provided below.

Table 3:5

Jill's Panic Sequence

Panic #	Sequence
1.	a. at home watching TV
	b. felt heart flutter
	c. focused on my heart and worried about heart attack
	d. heart rate sped up
	e. convinced I was in danger
	f. called my husband and asked him to come home
2.	a. in restaurant with family
	b. thought "what would happen if I panicked here - I'd be really embarrassed"
	c. began to feel numb all over
	d. thought I would panic and have to run out of the restaurant
	e. lost my appetite
	f. asked husband and son to eat quickly so we could leave
3.	a. in shopping mall
	b. felt dizzy and lightheaded
	c. looked for exit and felt trapped
	d. walked quickly to end of mall
	e. heart rate speeding
	f. thought I would faint

Do the same kind of sequence analyses for three of your recent panic attacks in the space provided.

Table 3:6

Panic Sequence for Recent Panic Attacks

Panic #   Sequence

1.
   a. _____
   b. _____
   c. _____
   d. _____
   e. _____
   f. _____

2.
   a. _____
   b. _____
   c. _____
   d. _____
   e. _____
   f. _____

3.
   a. _____
   b. _____
   c. _____
   d. _____
   e. _____
   f. _____

How Does It All Begin

As we noted above, understanding the causes of extreme anxiety or panic attacks is not necessary in order to benefit from treatment, but it is helpful. It is not necessary because factors that are involved in the onset of a problem are not necessarily the same as the factors involved in the maintenance of the problem. For example, one may initially panic during the stress of a marital separation but then continue to panic even after the marital problems have been resolved.

A lot of people ask if there are genetic factors in anxiety and panic; that is, do you inherit anxiety and panic? This is an area of research advancing quickly. It seems that there is an inherited component to being anxious or tense but this does not necessarily mean that you inherit a problem with anxiety or a specific anxiety disorder. That is, one does not inherit the disorder of agoraphobia or simple phobia, for example. However, a general sensitivity, which is probably inherited, does seem to play a role. A generalized sensitivity or strong emotional reactivity to events that happen in one's life may involve both anxious and nonanxious moods. Therefore, having sensitivity, being someone who is emotional and sensitive to good and bad news, is not necessarily a sign of impending anxiety. However, it does seem that a general sensitivity or being "high strung" may underlie many of the anxiety disorders. When combined with other factors this sensitivity can contribute to the development of an anxiety problem.

As we mentioned above, panic attacks typically first occur in the context of a stressful life event. Stress can arise from negative events (such as loss of a job, illness in the family, financial difficulty, physical ill health, etc.) and from positive events (e.g., marriage, a new baby, job promotion, purchasing/building a home). During these periods of time, individuals are sensitized in a way that makes them more susceptible to panic attacks with minimal provocation. Now, not everyone who is under stress or is anxious develops panic attacks. Some people develop other problems such as headaches, hypertension, ulcers, or nervous stomachs (irritable bowel syndrome). In fact, there is some evidence that these type of problems also run in families and may be inherited! For example, if your parents, or others in your family develop headaches when they are tense, the chances are greater that you will also have headaches. Similarly, if panic attacks run in your family, the chances are greater that you will experience panic also if under stress. If you are high strung, anxious, or tense to begin with, then you have a greater chance of developing nervous stomach or panic attacks. But this does not mean that anxiety or panic is inherited in the same way that hair or eye color is inherited. You may inherit a tendency (called a vulnerability) to be anxious or to panic without ever becoming anxious or panicking because you think and act in ways that prevent it from happening. Of course, we're not even sure yet if the tendency or vulnerability to have panic attacks is inherited. It may be simply that you watched your parents panic in stressful situations and now you do as well.

In any case, a person sensitized by stress can encounter a situation which, under less stressful times, would cause them to feel very little anxiety and no panic attacks but now they panic. This first attack may be followed by other panic attacks in various places or situations due to generalization, which we will discuss in the next lesson. The way in which the cycle of anxiety and panic continues will be described in more detail, but it is important at the moment for you to realize that panic attacks are in many ways just like other manifestations of stress (headaches and ulcers) and often develop in the context of stressful circumstances.

Training Program Rationale

This program will teach you to alter your responses by learning to change the way you think and the way you react physically and behaviorally to particular events. In essence, the program involves learning new methods of control. At present, you are most likely intensifying your anxiety because of the "anxious" nature of your thoughts and the "activation" of your physical nervous system.

This program consists of three basic strategies: techniques designed to modify what you say to yourself (your self-statements), techniques designed to control your physical sensations, and techniques designed to help you face more comfortably the things that you currently fear and avoid. As you learn to master the procedures, you will be much better able to understand anxiety and panic and to deal with anxiety and panic in a wide range of situations.

We will begin with the cognitive strategies directed at your thinking or self-statements. Due to the interactive nature of the components of anxiety and panic, changing your thoughts will in turn affect to some extent your physiology and your behavior. However, we also include treatments that focus directly upon those aspects. The cognitive strategies will involve a detailed understanding of panic attacks and looking for the specific kinds of misinterpretations that can contribute to anxiety and panic. You will be taught methods of questioning and challenging your interpretations and assumptions. Once you are able to isolate the particular self-statements that often precipitate anxiety and panic, you will learn to treat them as beliefs or hypotheses rather than as facts. The general strategy is to question and challenge these hypotheses by examining the evidence and examining how you arrived at the conclusions.

The second aspect of the treatment involves teaching you techniques to help you directly control many of your physical sensations. This will be done through control of your breathing and muscle tension. Many people breathe too much when they have a panic attack even though it often feels like the opposite (not enough oxygen). Overbreathing is often one of the major reasons for the physical sensations that are experienced. Thus, learning to control your breathing will help to reduce many of the panic symptoms. In addition, muscle relaxation is used as a strategy of maintaining physiological calmness if you feel yourself getting uptight.

The third part of this treatment involves examining the sensations which have become part of your panic response and helping you to repeatedly experience those sensations in a way that replaces your fear with a nonfearful reaction. In this way, you will learn to deal with panic that seems to come out of the blue and with the anticipation of future panic.

The fourth part of the treatment entails exposure or practice in the situations that you have been avoiding because they have in the past become associated with anxiety and panic. Again, you will learn to deal with the fear in those situations.

It is important to realize that achieving control of your anxiety and panic is a skill that has to be learned. To be effective, these skills must be practiced regularly.

Exercise

Your assignment for this week is to continue to monitor your anxiety and panic, looking for patterns of response and identifying possible triggers, for one week. Use the PANIC ATTACK RECORD and DAILY MOOD RECORD. In addition, it will be important for you to write down something else about your panic attacks. For each panic attack that occurs, keep a record of the sequence of events that led up to the panic just as you did before for recent panic attacks. Do this in the space provided below (Table 3:7). It may seem that panic attacks occur all at once, but if you step back and observe, you will discover a sequential process.

Self-Assessment

Answer by circling true (T) or false (F). Answers are on page A-1.

1. Anxiety and panic are <u>reactions</u> made up of three major   T   F
    components: physiology, thoughts and behaviors.

2. One should never feel anxious.   T   F

3. Physiology, thoughts and behaviors interact and   T   F
    spiral the emotional state.

4. Heredity explains all of panic.   T   F

5. Anxiety is different from panic - anxiety is usually   T   F
    anticipation of future events while panic is a sudden
    rush of fear.

Table 3:7

Panic Sequences

Panic #	Sequence
1.	a. _____
	b. _____
	c. _____
	d. _____
	e. _____
	f. _____
2.	a. _____
	b. _____
	c. _____
	d. _____
	e. _____
	f. _____
3.	a. _____
	b. _____
	c. _____
	d. _____
	e. _____
	f. _____

CHAPTER 4

What Produces the Panic Feelings

Review of Records

Look back over your weekly monitoring of DAILY MOOD and PANIC ATTACKS. Examine the patterns of occurrence of the panic attacks. Has more information emerged from your second week of monitoring? Does the panic occur in particular circumstances? What is the first symptom you typically notice when the panic begins? Analyze the sequence of events from your panic sequence record. What tends to be the first response, the second, what follows, and how do the different responses spiral into a panic? Complete the second week of your PROGRESS RECORD by adding the average anxiety and number of panics over the last week to the chart. Connect those two points with a line. Do not be concerned at this time if the line has not shown a reduction. Reduction in panic and anxiety does not typically occur overnight, as changing your reactions is a learning process that occurs with time and practice.

The Physiology of Panic

While panic, by definition and nature, is an unpleasant experience, it is not in the least dangerous. Panic is a response to danger or threat. Scientifically, panic is termed the fight or flight response or the emergency reaction. It is so named because all of its effects are aimed towards dealing with an emergency by either fighting or fleeing the danger. Thus, the number one purpose of panic is to protect the organism. Back in the days when our ancestors lived in caves, it was vital that when faced with some overwhelming present danger, an automatic response would take over causing us to take immediate action, to attack or run. Even in today's hectic world this is a necessary mechanism. Just imagine if you were crossing the street when suddenly a car sped towards you blasting its horn. If you experienced absolutely no anxiety, you would be killed. However, most likely, your fight/flight response would take over and you would run out of the way to safety. The moral of this story is a simple one — the purpose of panic is to protect the organism, not to harm it. It would be totally nonsensical for nature to develop a mechanism whose purpose is to protect an organism, and yet in so doing, harms it.

Thus, the best way to think of all of the components of panic (the behavior, the physiology and the thoughts) is to remember that they are all aimed at getting the organism prepared for immediate action and that their purpose is protection. When it is working correctly, let's say after you have jumped out of the way of a car, you will collect yourself and make a mental note and be sure and look both ways at that particular corner in the future and then go about your business. You would not start worrying about your heart beating too fast or your palpitations. However, if you have this response and there is nothing to fear, then it is a panic attack. Since you don't know why it's happening, the attack can elicit more anxiety and fear and spiral into a terrifying experience. This is particularly true if something has made you worry about being sick to begin with. For example, did a member of your family recently die of a heart attack? Was your mother always concerned about your health while you were growing up? If so, then health related concerns may be in the back of your mind, and it is only natural that you start thinking about heart attacks or other physical dangers when your body speeds up and feels out of control during a panic attack. It is, therefore, important to understand the physiology of panic.

a)   Nervous and Chemical Effects

When some sort of danger is perceived or anticipated, the brain sends messages to a section of your nerves called the autonomic nervous system. The autonomic nervous system has two subsections or branches called the sympathetic nervous system and the parasympathetic nervous system. It is these two branches of the nervous system which are directly involved in controlling the body's energy levels in preparation for action. Very simply put, the sympathetic nervous system is the emergency fight/flight response system which releases energy and gets the body primed for action while the parasympathetic nervous system is the restoring system which returns the body to a normal state.

One important point is that the sympathetic nervous system tends to be largely an all or none system. That is, when it is activated, all of its parts respond. In other words, either all the symptoms are experienced or no symptoms are experienced; it is rare for changes to occur in one part of the body alone. This may explain why most panic attacks involve many symptoms and not just one or two.

One of the major effects of the sympathetic nervous system is that it releases two chemicals called adrenalin and noradrenalin from the adrenal glands on the kidneys. These chemicals in turn are used as messengers by the sympathetic nervous system to continue activity so that once activity in the sympathetic nervous system begins, it often continues and increases for a period of time. However, it is very important to note that sympathetic nervous system activity is stopped in two ways. First, the chemical messengers, adrenalin and noradrenalin, are eventually destroyed by other chemicals in the body. Second, the parasympathetic nervous system (which generally has opposing effects to the sympathetic nervous system) becomes activated and restores a relaxed state. It is very important to realize that eventually the body will have enough of the emergency response and will activate the parasympathetic nervous system to restore a state of relaxation. In other words, anxiety arousal cannot continue forever and not spiral to ever increasing and possibly damaging levels. The parasympathetic nervous system is a built in protector which stops the sympathetic nervous system from getting carried away. Another important point is that the chemical messengers, adrenalin and noradrenalin, take some time to be completely destroyed. Thus, even after the immediate danger and accompanying surge of emotion has passed and your sympathetic nervous system has stopped responding, you are likely to feel keyed up or apprehensive for some time because the chemicals are still floating around in your system. You must remind yourself that this is perfectly natural and harmless. In fact, this is an adaptive function because, in the wild, danger often has a habit of returning and it is useful for the organism to be prepared to reactivate the emergency response. In other words, the sensations that you experience during panic and that can become frightening in and of themselves are real sensations — there is no attempt being made here to say that the sensations are all in your mind. They are real and they are physiologically based. The question becomes why did they arise in the first place, which we will discuss later.

b)   Cardiovascular Effects

Activity in the parasympathetic nervous system produces an increase in heart rate and in the strength of the heartbeat. This is vital to preparation for action since it helps speed up the blood flow, thus improving delivery of the oxygen to the tissues and the removal of waste products from the tissues. In addition to increased activity in the heart, there is also a change in blood flow. Basically, the blood is redirected away from the places where it is not needed by a tightening of the blood vessels (usually away from the periphery) and towards the places where it is needed more, by an expansion of blood vessels (usually toward the big muscle groups in the legs, etc). For example, blood is taken away from the skin, fingers and toes. Not only is this useful as a survival function for permitting more action of the central organs, but also because if the organism is attacked and cut in the peripheral body parts, it is less likely to bleed to death. Hence, during panic and, to a certain extent during anxiety, the skin looks pale and cold, and the fingers and toes become cold and sometimes feel numb and prickly or tingly.

c)   Respiratory Effects

The emergency response is associated with an increase in the speed and depth of breathing. This has obvious importance for the defense of the organism since the tissues need to get more oxygen to prepare for action. The feelings produced by this increase in breathing, however, can include breathlessness, choking or smothering sensations, and even pain and tightness in the chest. As a side effect of increased breathing, especially if no actual activity occurs, the blood supply to the head is decreased. While this is only a small amount and is not at all dangerous, it produces a collection of unpleasant symptoms such as dizziness, blurred vision, confusion, etc. We will be discussing the role of respiratory effects and the physiological basis in more detail next lesson.

d)   Sweat Gland Effects

Activation of the emergency response produces an increase in sweating. This has important adaptive functions such as cooling the body to stop it from overheating and making the skin more slippery so that it is more difficult for a predator to grab.

e)   Other Physical Effects

A number of other effects are produced by activation of the arousal system, none of which are in any way harmful. For example, the pupils widen or dilate to let in more light and extend peripheral vision, to look for danger, which may in turn result in sensitivity to light, or spots in front of the eyes. There is often a decrease in salivation and a decrease in digestive processes in general, resulting in a dry mouth. The decrease in the digestive system often produces nausea, a heavy feeling in the stomach and even constipation. Many of the muscle groups tense up in preparation and this results in subjective feelings of tension, sometimes extending to pains and aches as well as trembling and shaking.

Overall, the emergency response results in general activation of the whole bodily metabolism and an increased sensitivity to stimulation from the external environment. One often feels hot and flushed. Because this whole process takes a lot of energy, the person generally feels tired, drained and washed out afterwards.

As mentioned before, the emergency response prepares the body for action to either attack or run. Thus, it is no surprise that the overwhelming urge associated with this response is to escape wherever you are. You may have had the thoughts "I've got to get out of here." When escape is not possible because you're in church in the middle of the pew or at an important meeting, the urges will often become stronger or be shown through such behaviors as foot tapping, pacing or snapping at people.

Cognitively, the number one effect of the emergency response is to alert the organism to the possible existence of danger. Thus, one of the major effects is an immediate and automatic shift in attention to search the surroundings for potential threat. This is a normal and important part of the emergency response since its purpose is to stop you from attending to your ongoing chores and to permit you to scan your surroundings for danger. Sometimes an obvious threat cannot be found. Most of us cannot accept having no explanation for something. Therefore, in many cases, when people cannot find an explanation for their sensations, they turn their search inwards upon themselves. In other words, if there is nothing that makes me feel anxious, then there must be something wrong with me. Then, the brain "invents" an explanation such as I must be dying, losing control, or going crazy. As we have seen, nothing could be further from the truth since the purpose of the fight/flight response is to protect the organism and not harm it. Nevertheless, these are understandable thoughts.

But How Does Panic Occur

Up until now, we have looked at the components of anxiety and panic and seen how these components may interact to spiral anxiety and panic, but we haven't looked at why the fight/flight response is activated when there is nothing to be frightened of. Why is it continually activated?

Following extensive research, it appears that what people with panic attacks are frightened of are the actual physical sensations of the emergency response. Panic attacks can be seen as a sequence. First, you experience a set of unexpected physical symptoms characteristic of the emergency response and second, you become frightened. The second part of this sequence is easy to understand. As discussed earlier, the emergency response causes the brain to search for danger. When an obvious external danger cannot be found, the mind looks inward and "invents" a reason, such as I am dying or losing control. As we noted above, if thoughts of illness or heart attacks are in the back of your mind anyway, it is understandable that this is the danger that is focused upon. Obviously, such thoughts lead to additional anxiety and additional anxiety leads to further intensification of the arousal mechanism and physical symptoms. Of course, after a number of repetitions of the panic experience, the anxiety and fear can occur in response to the initial physical sensations without any conscious mediating thoughts of danger, which is what makes panic seem automatic, unpredictable or out of the blue. That is, sometimes you may be aware of thoughts of danger (e.g., "I'm having a heart attack"), but for other attacks you may not be directly aware of any dangerous thoughts or even any sensations that might have triggered the panic. When this happens, the attacks seem even more unpredictable and uncontrollable. However, keep in mind that the cues which elicit panic reactions are always present, even if not immediately obvious.

The first part of the model is harder to understand. Why do you experience the physical symptoms of the emergency response if you are not frightened to begin with? This is where stress comes in. For example, as we mentioned above, if you have become generally stressed for some reason in your life, this stress results in an increase in the production of adrenalin and other chemicals which from time to time produce symptoms. This is your body's way of staying alert and prepared to deal with the stress or take some action. But one of the courses of action is the emergency response. Thus, stress alone can trigger an emergency response especially in people who have experienced frightening or uncontrollable events often enough earlier in life. Thus, feeling stressed along with the chemical reaction of stress, can set off the emergency response even when there is no emergency. This is particularly true if you are somehow vulnerable to react to stress in this way as we discussed above.

The other important point is that once the anticipation of panic has begun, which in turn tends to create higher levels of physical stress and more physical symptoms of stress, one becomes very vigilant for the signals of impending panic (i.e., the physical symptoms). That is, you may be scanning your body for strange or frightening physical feelings and picking up on sensations that you might not have otherwise noticed. As you can see, a cycle of anticipation and vigilance, symptoms and panic, more anticipation and so on, begins.

Thus, the final model of panic attacks in a simplified way looks like this:

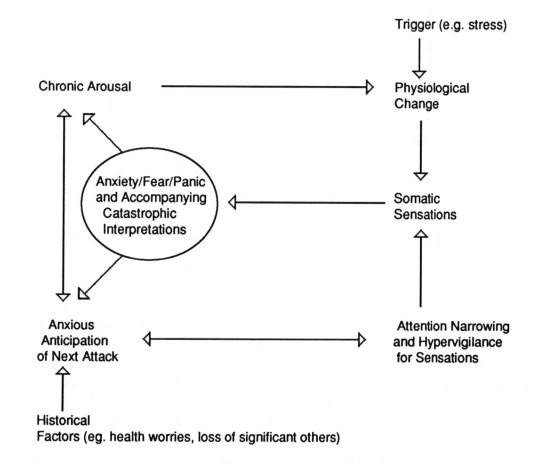

In summary then, panic is scientifically known as the emergency response since its primary purpose is to activate the organism and protect it from harm. Everyone is capable of this response when confronted with danger.

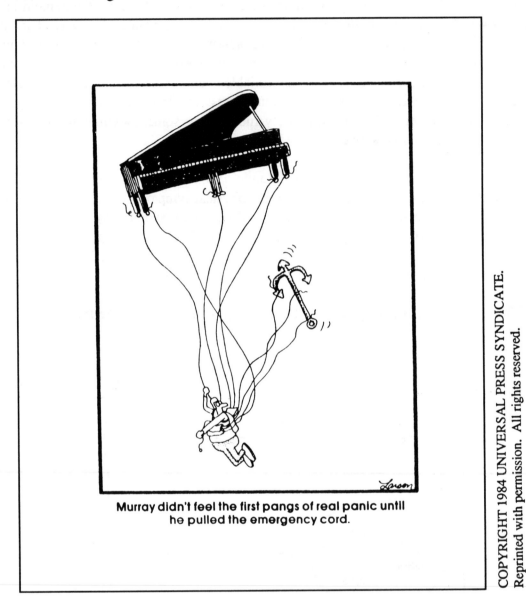

Murray didn't feel the first pangs of real panic until he pulled the emergency cord.

Associated with this response are a number of physical, behavioral and mental changes. Importantly, once the danger has gone, many of these changes can continue, especially the physical ones, almost with a mind of their own, due to learning and other longer term chronic arousal effects. When physical symptoms occur in the absence of an obvious explanation, people often misinterpret the normal emergency symptoms as indicating a serious physical or mental problem. In this case, the sensations themselves can often become threatening and can trigger the whole emergency response again. It is, therefore, important to recognize that there are certain myths and misinterpretations about the emergency response and to know the most common ones. While we will be discussing each of these myths in more detail later as they relate to your own panic reaction, here is a review of some of the most common misinterpretations that people have. Unfortunately, such myths serve only to intensify the anxious anticipation and panicky feelings.

1. <u>Going crazy</u>

Many people believe that when they experience the physical symptoms of the emergency response, they are going crazy. They are most likely referring to the severe mental disorder known as schizophrenia. Let us look at schizophrenia to see how likely this is. Schizophrenia is a major disorder characterized by such severe symptoms as disjointed thoughts and speech, sometimes extending to nonsensical speech, delusions or strange beliefs and hallucinations. Examples of the strange beliefs might be the receiving of messages from out of space, and examples of hallucinations might be the hearing of voices that are not really there.

Schizophrenia generally begins very gradually and not suddenly such as during a panic. Additionally, because it runs strongly in families and has a genetic base, only a certain proportion of people can become schizophrenic and in other people no amount of stress will cause the disorder. A third important point is that people who become schizophrenic usually show some mild symptoms for most of their lives (such as unusual thoughts, flowery speech, etc.). Thus, if this has not been noticed yet in you, then the chances are that you will not become schizophrenic. This is especially true if you are over 25 years of age since schizophrenia generally first appears in the late teens to early 20's. Finally, if you have been through interviews with a psychologist or psychiatrist, then you can be fairly certain that you would know by now if you are likely to become schizophrenic.

2. <u>Losing Control</u>

Some people believe they are "going to lose control when they panic." Presumably, they mean that they will become totally paralyzed and not be able to move, or that they will not know what they are doing and will run around wild, hurting people or yelling out obscenities and embarrassing themselves. Alternatively, they may not know what to expect but may just experience an overwhelming feeling that something bad is going to happen.

From our earlier discussion, it can be seen where this feeling comes from. During the emergency response, the entire body is ready for action and there is an overwhelming desire to escape. However, the emergency response is not aimed at hurting other people who are not a threat and will not produce paralysis. Rather, the entire response is simply aimed at getting you away from potential danger. There has never been a recorded case of someone going "wild" during a panic. Even though the emergency response makes you feel somewhat confused, unreal and distracted when you are not actually <u>using</u> the response, as in jumping out of the way of a car, you are still able to think and function normally. Ironically, if you <u>are</u> using the response, you are able to think faster and more clearly, and you are actually physically stronger and your reflexes are quicker. Think of examples of mothers dealing with very frightening situations very well because they are trying to save their children. A client who attended our clinic initially had a strong fear of losing control. She reported that on one occasion she had panicked when driving to a job interview, and so she changed direction and headed for her husband's office instead. She reported that this was loss of control. On the contrary, she was in complete control as she was functioning to escape the situation of being alone and was directing her behavior towards that escape. There was no doubt that she was engaging in unadaptive behavior because there was no real threat but she incorrectly interpreted that as a loss of control.

3. Nervous Collapse

Many people are frightened by beliefs that their nerves might become exhausted and they may collapse. As discussed earlier, the emergency response is produced chiefly through activity in the sympathetic nervous system which is counteracted by the parasympathetic nervous system. The parasympathetic nervous system is, in a sense, a safeguard to protect against the possibility that the sympathetic nervous system may become "worn out." Nerves are not like electrical wires and anxiety cannot wear out, damage, or use up nerves. The absolute worst that could happen during a panic attack is that an individual could pass out at which point the sympathetic nervous system would stop its over-activity and the person would regain consciousness within a few seconds. However, actually passing out as a result of the emergency response is quite rare, and if it does occur, it is adaptive since it is a way for the body to return to normal. Another concern is that by repeated panic and anxiety, the chances of future nervous collapse are increased. However, again, anxiety does not physically wear out your nerves and there is even some evidence to suggest that by repeated experiences of stress and anxiety you may toughen or strengthen your nervous system. For example, in times of severe national crisis or disaster such as war, the incidents of psychological problems do not increase, but instead there seems to be a toughening up to deal with the stress.

4. Heart Attacks

Many people misinterpret the symptoms of the emergency response and believe that they must be dying of a heart attack. This is probably because many people do not have enough knowledge about heart attacks. Let us look at the facts of heart disease and see how this differs from panic attacks. The major symptoms of heart disease are breathlessness and chest pain, as well as occasional palpitations and fainting. The symptoms in heart disease are generally directly related to effort. That is, the harder you exercise, the worse the symptoms and the less you exercise, the better the symptoms. The symptoms usually go away fairly quickly with rest. This is very different from the symptoms associated with panic attacks which often occur at rest and "seem to have a mind of their own." Certainly, panic symptoms can occur during exercise or can intensify during exercise, but they are different from the symptoms of a heart attack since they can occur equally often at rest. Of most importance, heart disease will almost always produce major electrical changes in the heart which are picked up very obviously by an electrocardiogram (EKG). In panic attacks, the only change which shows up on an EKG is an increase in heart rate. Thus, if you have had an EKG and the doctor has given you the all clear, you can safely assume that heart disease is not the cause of your attacks.

Think of any other major fears that you have in anticipation of a panic attack or when experiencing a panic attack. Sometimes it is difficult to identify these thoughts because they become almost habit-like. If you are frightened of the feeling of panic, ask yourself why, and what are the consequences that you believe could happen if you panic. We will be working through these questions in more detail in the following lessons but start to ask yourself those questions now. Do you hold any of the myths that were described above? If you hold those myths, despite evidence to suggest that they are not accurate, imagine how those beliefs contribute to the spiral of responding that we described earlier and lead to the feeling of panic.

It is important to understand where misinterpretations originate. As mentioned previously, we tend to look for an external cause for the sense of danger and when that is not apparent, it would seem logical to look internally and attribute the panic to some physical or mental problem. The specific content of the attribution can be influenced by information given to you from other people. For example, we have come across a dictionary definition of panic (in a reputable medical guide) as a state that can lead into psychotic depression. That is misinformation, as there is no evidence to suggest that sequence of events. However, for someone like yourself who has not had a background in psychological research, that kind of information could very easily provide the basis for a strong fear of becoming psychotic when panicking. If someone is continuously afraid of becoming psychotic when panicking, then it is very understandable that the experience of panic is terrifying and that there is a constant anxious anticipation of panic and an attempt to avoid provocation of panicking.

Attempts to avoid panic can occur in several ways, including avoidance of situations in which a panic has occurred or situations similar to those in which panic has occurred in the past. By association and certain attributional processes or expectancies, people begin to expect to panic in those situations. Similarly, certain activities that bring on the physical feelings connected with the feelings experienced during panic, including activities such as drinking coffee, watching a horror movie, or engaging in physical exercise, may be avoided. Unfortunately, constantly hoping to keep panic at bay simply adds tension.

Exercise

In order to integrate the information that has been given to you in this lesson, which in many cases may be very different from the kind of understanding that you had, it is essential that you read through this material several times before beginning the next lesson. Allow yourself time to integrate the information thoroughly, to understand very well the conceptualization of what is panic and the basis for the physiological reactions that occur during panic. In addition, as you do your monitoring over the week, using your DAILY MOOD RECORD and PANIC ATTACK RECORD, keep a very close watch on the kinds of thoughts that you have in the back of your mind related to either the anticipation of panic or the experience of panic. Allow yourself a full week of integrating this lesson's information and understanding your anxiety and panic before continuing with the next lesson.

Self-Assessment

Answer each of the following by circling true (T) or false (F). Answers are on page A-2.

1. A panic attack is a medical problem over which you have no control.   T   F

2. The symptoms experienced during panic, such as racing heart and sweating, indicate a physical disease process that is dangerous.   T   F

3. Panic is an emergency response which is primarily a protective mechanism.   T   F

4. Panics that seem to occur from out of the blue often can be related to specific subtle events such as changes in breathing patterns or excitement from other events.   T   F

5. When the body is activated into a panic reaction, it could go on for ever and ever.   T   F

6. People do not go crazy when they panic.   T   F

CHAPTER 5

Learning Physical Control

Review of Records

Examine your PANIC ATTACK and DAILY MOOD records over the past week. Have any further patterns emerged from your monitoring? Have your panic attacks become more understandable in terms of the sequence of responding that spirals? Have you been able to identify certain patterns of thoughts which may feed into the panic cycle? Have you noticed additional situations or activities that you avoid because of the anticipation of panic? Add your monitoring data (average anxiety and number of panic attacks over the past week) to your PROGRESS RECORD.

Control of Physical Sensations

In this session you are going to learn how to modify some of the symptoms of which you are frightened. The first type of panic-related physical symptoms that we will address are breathing symptoms. It has been established that 50-60% of people who panic show some signs of overbreathing or hyperventilation. Overbreathing may serve to either produce an initial symptom to which you react with panic, and/or it may develop as part of the panic reaction after the fear has begun. It will be necessary for you to decide whether overbreathing is an important part of your panics. If hyperventilation is not part of your reaction, then an alternative method of controlling your physical sensations is deep relaxation, which is discussed later in this lesson. There are several ways of determining whether hyperventilating is part of your reaction. First, answer the following questions:

1. In general, do you often feel short of breath as if you are
    not getting enough air?   Y__ N __

2. Do you sometimes feel as if you are suffocating?   Y__ N __

3. Do you experience chest pain, tingling, and prickling and
    numbness sensations?   Y__ N __

4. Do you yawn or sigh a lot or take in big gulps of air?   Y__ N __

5. When you are frightened, do you hold your breath or
    breathe very quickly and shallow?   Y__ N __

If you answered yes to any of those questions, then it is likely that overbreathing plays a part in your panic reactions. Of course, if you're like many people, you may not be aware of your breathing patterns. Therefore, it is important to test yourself.

Try a small exercise. Sit in a comfortable chair and breathe very fast and very deep as if you are blowing up a balloon. Try to continue for a minute and a half, but stop before that if you wish. When doing this exercise, it is important that you exhale very hard and take the air right down to your lungs. Be very forceful and deep in your breathing. Once you have finished the exercise, close your eyes and breathe slowly, pausing at the end of each breath. Continue the slow breathing for one to two minutes until any symptoms have abated. Now, think about the symptoms you experienced. Check off the symptoms from one of your PANIC ATTACK RECORDS. Did you experience symptoms which are similar to the ones that you experience when you panic? It is possible that the fear level was not the same as when you panic because you know how the symptoms developed, but were the physical symptoms similar to naturally occurring panic attacks? If there was a big overlap, then this would be a very good indicator that hyperventilation or overbreathing does play a role in your panic attacks. If the symptoms were not similar, try the overbreathing procedure again, but this time continue for two to two and a half minutes. At the end, again assess whether the symptoms were similar to those that you experience naturally. If not, then it is likely that overbreathing is not significant in your panics and it would be more appropriate to use another method of controlling physical symptoms, such as relaxation techniques, and you may skip the next section and proceed onto relaxation training. If the symptoms you experienced from this exercise are similar to the symptoms you experience when you become frightened, continue with this section for breathing retraining. Some people find that they get something out of both breathing retraining and relaxation. There is certainly nothing wrong with doing both. However, the worst thing you could do is to try the exercises half-heartedly. Whether you do one or both, you must put in your full effort to get the benefits.

Breathing Physiology

Before learning the correct method of breathing, it is important to understand the basis for the effects of overbreathing. The body needs oxygen in order to survive. Whenever a person inhales, oxygen is taken into the lungs where it is picked up by the hemoglobin (the "oxygen sticky" chemical in the blood). The hemoglobin carries the oxygen around the body where it is released for use by the cells. The cells use the oxygen in their energy reactions, subsequently producing a bi-product called carbon dioxide (CO_2), which is, in turn, released back into the blood, transported to the lungs, and exhaled.

Efficient control of the body's energy reactions depends on the maintenance of a specific balance between oxygen and CO_2. This balance can be maintained chiefly through an appropriate rate and depth of breathing. Obviously, breathing "too much" will have the effect of increasing levels of oxygen (in the blood only) and decreasing levels of CO_2 because the oxygen is not used at the same rate that it is taken in. Breathing too little will have the effect of decreasing levels of oxygen and increasing levels of CO_2. The appropriate rate of breathing, at rest, is usually around 10 to 14 breaths per minute.

Hyperventilation is defined as a rate and depth of breathing which is too much for the body's needs at a particular point in time. Naturally, if the need for oxygen and the production of CO_2 both increase (such as during exercise), breathing should increase appropriately. Alternately, if the need for oxygen and the production of CO_2 both decrease (such as during relaxation), breathing should decrease appropriately.

While most of the body's mechanisms are controlled by "automatic" chemical and physical means, and breathing is no exception, breathing has an additional property of being able to be put under voluntary control. For example, it is quite easy for us to hold our breath such as when swimming underwater, or to speed up our breathing when blowing up a balloon. Therefore, a number of "non-automatic" factors such as emotion, stress or habit can cause us to increase our breathing. These factors may be especially important in people who suffer panic attacks.

Interestingly, while most of us consider oxygen to be the determining factor in our breathing, the body actually uses CO_2 as its "marker" for appropriate breathing. The most important effect of overbreathing then is to produce a marked drop in CO_2. This, in turn, produces a drop in the acid content of the blood leading to what is known as alkaline blood. It is these two effects — a decrease in blood CO_2 content and an increase in blood alkalinity — which are responsible for most of the physical changes that occur during overbreathing.

One of the most important changes produced by hyperventilation is a constriction or narrowing of certain blood vessels around the body. In particular, the blood going to the brain is somewhat decreased. Coupled together with this tightening of blood vessels is the fact that the hemoglobin increases its "stickiness" for oxygen. Thus, not only does less blood reach certain areas of the body but the oxygen carried by this blood is less likely to be released to the tissues. Paradoxically, then, while overbreathing means we are taking in more oxygen, we are actually getting less oxygen to certain areas of our brain and body. This effect results in two broad categories of symptoms: (1) centrally, symptoms are produced by the slight reduction in oxygen to certain parts of the brain (including dizziness, lightheadedness, confusion, breathlessness, blurred vision, and unreality); (2) peripherally, some symptoms are produced by the slight reduction in oxygen to certain parts of the body (including an increase in heart rate to pump more blood around, numbness and tingling in the extremities, cold, clammy hands and sometimes stiffness of the muscles). It is important to remember that the reductions in oxygen are slight and totally harmless. It is also important to point out that overbreathing (possibly due to a reduction in oxygen to a certain part of the brain) can produce a feeling of breathlessness, sometimes extending to feelings of choking or smothering, so that it actually feels as if one is not getting enough air. However, that is in contrast to what is actually happening.

Hyperventilation or overbreathing is also responsible for a number of overall effects. First, the act of overbreathing is hard physical work. Hence, it often produces a feeling of being hot, flushed, and sweaty. Second, because it is hard work to overbreathe, prolonged periods will often result in tiredness and exhaustion. Third, people who overbreathe often tend to breathe from their chest rather than their diaphragm (the muscle underneath the lungs, central to the base of the rib cage). This means that their chest muscles tend to become tired and tense, resulting in symptoms of chest pressure and tightness, like a band pulling around the chest or even severe chest pain. Finally, many people who overbreathe tend to engage in a habit of repeatedly sighing or yawning. These patterns are actually forms of hyperventilation since whenever one yawns or sighs, a large quantity of CO_2 is dumped very quickly. Therefore, when combating the problem, it is important to become aware of habitual sighing and yawning and to try to suppress these habits.

You might say that you indeed experience a lot of these symptoms but that you don't hyperventilate or that you don't gasp for air. In many cases, hyperventilation can be very subtle. This is especially true if the person has been slightly overbreathing for a long period of time. In this case, there can be marked drops in CO_2 but, due to compensation in the body, relatively little change in the alkalinity occurs. The compensation prevents symptoms from being produced. However, because CO_2 levels are kept low, the body loses some of its ability to cope with changes in CO_2 so that even a slight change in breathing, such as through a yawn, can be enough to suddenly trigger symptoms. This may account for the sudden nature of many panics.

Probably the most important point to be made about hyperventilation is that it is not dangerous. In fact, forced hyperventilation is a medical test that is commonly requested of patients. Breathing patterns are an integral part of the emergency response and thus, are intended to protect the body from danger rather than be dangerous. The changes associated with hyperventilating are those which prepare the body for action in order to escape potential external harm as noted earlier. If fleeing or fighting actually occurred, a state of overbreathing or hyperventilation would not develop since the oxygen would be used at the rate that it is taken in. However, hyperventilating is not dangerous. Nevertheless, it is an understandable reaction for the brain to immediately expect danger and for the individual to feel the urge to escape once acute hyperventilation has begun.

Breathing Control

Once you fully understand the reasons and basis of overbreathing, the next step is to learn the technique of breathing retraining. This is a skill and, therefore, takes several weeks of practice. The reasons for rebreathing training are: (1) to eliminate some of the cues to which you are very sensitive and lead you to become fearful (i.e., the initial triggers for panic attack reactions); (2) to reduce physical symptoms during panics; and (3) to facilitate general relaxation which will reduce your levels of tension and, therefore, impede the unadaptive cycle of anticipation of panic and actual panic.

The exercise which we have found to be best involves basically two components. The first component is learning to slow your breathing. First, you must learn to think about your breathing while you breathe smoothly and normally. This is quite difficult for many people and you may find that when you initially start to think about and count your breathing, it begins to speed up. The reason for that is again a sensitivity to symptoms of overbreathing; because the overbreathing symptoms have been associated with a very fearful state of panic in the past, they subsequently become cues or signals of which you are afraid. Once you can think about your breathing, while maintaining a normal rate and depth, then you can begin to slow it down. The second component is a meditational one which helps you to strengthen your attention. Attention is very much like a muscle in your body and requires constant exercise to stay strong. Good attention is important since this will help you to slow your mind and concentrate on your breathing when you become anxious or panicky.

The following exercise is to be practiced two times, every day for a minimum of ten minutes each time. We recommend that you practice this exercise over the next week (7 days). If the exercise is difficult at first, don't stop because with practice it will become easier. Find yourself a quiet, comfortable spot where you will not be disturbed. Once you become good at controlling your breathing, you will be asked to practice anywhere at any time. However, initially it is best to practice in a quiet, comfortable area. Sit in a comfortable chair and allow yourself a few seconds to calm down. Now start to Count on your in-breaths. That is, when you breathe in think "one" to yourself.

As you breathe out, think the word "relax". Think "two" on your next breath in and "relax" on the breath out. Continue this up to the number ten and then back to number one. Ideally, you should think of nothing but your breathing and the words. This is very difficult for some people and you may never be able to do it perfectly. When you begin to do this exercise, you may not get past the first number without other thoughts coming into your mind. This is perfectly natural. When this happens, do not get angry or give up. Simply allow the thoughts to pass through your mind and bring your attention back to the numbers. You may have to practice this many times before you can concetrate fully on the exercise. Keep practicing and you will eventually find it easier.

At first, while you count each breath, breathe at your <u>USUAL RATE AND DEPTH</u>. Do not take in too much air and do not try to slow your breathing just yet. Just breathe smoothly and easily. To help you do this, place one hand on your chest and the other hand on your stomach with the little finger about one inch above the naval (belly button). Respiratory movement should come almost entirely from the lower (stomach) hand. Try to prevent the chest area from moving. If you are an habitual chest breather, this may feel very artificial and cause you some feeling of breathlessness. That is a natural response - just remember that you are indeed getting enough oxygen and the feelings of breathlessness will lessen the more your practice. If you find it extremely difficult to keep your chest still, lie down on the floor, flat on your stomach with your hands clasped under your head. This will make it easier to breathe from the diaphragm area. Once you have done that several times and feel comfortable breathing from the diaphragm, turn over and put a book on your stomach. Then, as you breathe in, try to raise the book. That is, every breath in should be accompanied by a ballooning out of the diaphragm and every breath out should be accompanied by a sucking in of the diaphragm. Try to keep your breathing <u>SMOOTH</u> and fluid. That is, don't gulp in a big breath and then let it out all at once. An additional hint is to breathe through your nose. This makes it more likely that you will breathe out slowly. It is not essential that you breathe through your nose but if you breathe through your mouth, try to keep the opening small so that you exhale slowly.

Now try the exercise described earlier where you count up to ten and back to one. After you have done that exercise, evaluate how it proceeded. Did you feel breathless or a little dizzy or did your breathing speed up as you began? If the symptoms felt very intense, you can stop the exercise for a while, calm down, and then <u>begin again</u>. It is just an indication of your sensitivity to the physical sensations which are associated with breathing. As you continue to do the exercise, the reactivity will diminish. Was it difficult for you to take in a breath right down to the diaphragm? If so, try to push your stomach out just before you breathe in so that there is space for the air to fill. Remember, however, not to take in more than your usual amount of air. And, remember to think of the air as oozing and escaping from your nose rather than being suddenly released when you exhale.

Practice this exercise every day, two times a day, for at least ten minutes each time, over the next seven days. Don't attempt to slow your breathing yet. Overall, it is most important that you practice regularly. If results are not immediate, do not despair. Remember that by learning this technique you are (1) learning to reduce symptoms which may be serving to cause you to become very frightened (i.e., the first cues in the sequence), and (2) learning to reduce overbreathing that occurs when you are frightened. At this point in time, you need not attempt to use this technique in specific situations or when you become frightened. First, it is important that you feel comfortable using the technique, so practice in a quiet, comfortable environment. An outline of the exercise is provided in Table 5:1.

Table 5:1

<u>Outline for Breathing Retraining</u>

<u>Stage 1</u>

1. Comfortable, quiet location.

2. Count "1" on breath in and think "relax" on breath out.
   Count "2" on breath in think "relax" on breath out, etc.

3. Focus attention on breathing and counting.

4. Normal rate and depth of breathing, using smooth
   inhalations and exhalations.

5. Expand diaphragm on breath in and keep chest still.

6. Count up to 10 and back to 1.

7. Practice twice daily, 10 minutes each time, for 7 days.

8. Monitor your practice.

After each practice, monitor your levels of concentration on the breathing exercise, and ease of breathing, using the BREATHING RETRAINING RECORD shown on the following page. Each form should last one week so feel free to tear out the form and make as many copies as you need. This will provide feedback for yourself and your doctor or mental health professional, if you're working with one.

<u>Muscle Relaxation Training</u>

For those of you for whom the breathing aspect does not seem to be at all relevant, learning muscle relaxation may be more appropriate, although some people will benefit from both. Tensing of the muscles is another component of the emotional states of anxiety and panic. It has an obvious survival value because muscle tension is a necessary step toward preparation for action. Obviously, it is very difficult to escape or run or fight off danger when you are in a very relaxed state. Muscle tension is also part of the general state of alertness and vigilance that characterizes general anxiety.

Try it. For one minute, tense your body as much as you can, without causing pain. Tense your legs, your arms, your face, your shoulders, your back, your stomach, tense everything. What are the effects of that kind of tension? It typically produces various sensations including tremor and shaking, weakness, pain in different parts of your body, fatigue, stiffening of the muscles, and sometimes a

TABLE 5:2

BREATHING RETRAINING RECORD

Rate concentration and breathing on 0 to 8 point scales

(where 0=none and 8=extremely good).

DATE	PRACTICE	CONCENTRATION DURING THE EXERCISE	EASE OF BREATHING
	1		
	2		
	1		
	2		
	1		
	2		
	1		
	2		
	1		
	2		
	1		
	2		
	1		
	2		

feeling of being immobilized. Assess whether the sensations you just experienced are at all similar to those you feel when anxious or panicky. Constant levels of tension can produce headaches, extreme tiredness, and other muscle body aches and pains. In other words, the state of tension can produce a whole range of sensations which in turn can become frightening in and of themselves because they are misinterpreted as being threatening and/or they have been associated with a feeling of anxiety or fear in the past. Because a strong connection exists between physical tension and a feeling of fear, it is understandable that awareness of muscular tension can produce feelings of being in danger or under threat, even if no real threat exists. Tension is part of the body's alertness and preparation for action, but if action does not take place, then the residual symptoms are much more noticeable.

The exercise which we find to be most helpful for both reducing general tension and as a method of reducing body tension when acutely frightened is called progressive muscle relaxation. This is a technique that was developed by a doctor named Jacobson a long time ago and has since proven very effective. It entails both releasing tension from major muscle groups in your body and focusing your attention on the sensations very objectively. You may find that as you initially focus on the relaxation procedure, you become frightened or feel as if you are losing control because deep relaxation does indeed produce sensations such as floating, heaviness or weakness. Those sensations might then act in the same way as do other physical symptoms when you become frightened. That is, initially, they could serve as cues of which you become frightened. If that happens, analyze it and appreciate that this is an example of your sensitivity which is out of proportion to any real danger. Therefore, as we will be seeing later, the primary method of getting over that sensitivity is repeated controlled exposures. In other words, feeling frightened at first by the relaxation procedure is an indication that the most important thing for you is to continue with the relaxation. The more you do it, the less uneasy and more relaxed you will feel.

Initially, the procedure takes about a half an hour because we work through 16 major muscle groups in the body. However, once you have become skilled in that method, the procedure is progressively shortened by focusing on eight muscle groups, then four muscle groups, and finally one-step relaxation.

The exercise entails initial tensing of the muscles followed by release or relaxation. The tensing has two purposes. First, the tension-relaxation mechanism is like a pendulum; the further you pull it one way, the further it will go the other. The more tension you produce, the easier it will be to relax. Secondly, purposeful tension enables you to become very aware of the differences in sensations produced by a state of tension versus a state of relaxation. This enhanced awareness will allow you to detect tension even at mild levels. Then, you will be in a better position to apply the relaxation technique as soon as you are aware of tension, instead of waiting for the tension to build up to high levels.

It is important to concentrate on your sensations in each part of your body during the exercise. It is easy for other thoughts to come into your mind. Try to let them pass through. Don't focus on them, and don't get angry or frustrated by them and give up. Just return your attention to the relaxation.

Begin by practicing the exercise in a quiet environment that is conducive to relaxation. Obviously, it will be important to subsequently practice in distracting environments, because you will need to be able to apply this skill wherever you are at times when you feel anxious. Therefore, the element of concentration is very important because, wherever you are, being able to focus on relaxing is essential to the effectiveness of this procedure. Find a quiet place and a very comfortable chair that provides support for your neck. If you don't have a comfortable, high-back chair, lie on your bed but do not fall asleep. Relaxation is indeed a very useful technique for people who have problems going to sleep, but in this case you are learning a method of control to be applied in daily life. It is not very adaptive to fall asleep when you begin to feel anxious in a shopping mall. Make sure that there are no pressure points on your body as you practice. That is, do not have your legs or arms crossed, and loosen tight shoes, belts, or restrictive clothing. Practice the relaxation at a time when you know you are not supposed to be doing something else. That is, devote a certain time every day just to the relaxation. Feeling that there are other things you should be doing is bound to create tension.

This exercise should be practiced every day, two times a day for the next seven days. Initially, that means 30 minutes two times a day. This is necessary in order to really benefit from the procedure because, as with the other techniques discussed, relaxation is a skill that requires practice in order to learn. Don't expect major changes initially. With practice, you will feel the effects of the relaxation.

Now, read the following set of instructions very carefully. Then, if possible, make a tape for yourself. That is, read the instructions onto the tape. Any cassette recorder or dictaphone will do. If you have a teenager, you probably can find one in their room. Find a comfortable position and play the tape back to yourself and follow the instructions. The tape will help initially, but as soon as you become very familiar with the procedures, the tape will not be necessary and you can practice on your own.

"Get into a comfortable position, close your eyes and sit quietly for a few seconds.

(1)   First, build up the tension in the lower arms by making fists with your hands and pulling up on the wrists. Feel the tension through the lower arms, the wrists, the fingers, the knuckles and the hands. Focus on the tension — notice the sensations of pulling, of discomfort, of tightness. Hold the tension for ten seconds. Now release the tension and let your hands and lower arms relax onto the chair or bed beside you, with the palms facing down. Focus your attention onto the sensations in your hands and arms. Feel the release from tension. Relax the muscles [twenty seconds.]

(2)   Now build up the tension in the upper arms by pulling the arms back and in towards your sides. Try not to tense muscles in other parts of your body, although there is obviously going to be some overlap. Feel the tension in the back of the arms radiating up into the shoulders and into your back. Focus on the sensations of tension. Hold the tension [ten seconds]. Now release the arms and let them relax heavily down. Focus on your upper arms and feel the difference in comparison to the tension. Your arms might feel heavy,

warm, and relaxed. [Relax for twenty seconds.]

(3)   Now build up the tension in the lower legs by flexing your feet and pulling your toes towards your upper body. Feel the tension as it spreads through your feet, your ankles, your shins, and your calf muscles. Feel the tension spreading down the back of the leg into the foot, under the foot and around the toes. Focus on that part of your body [ten seconds]. Now release the leg tension. Let your legs relax onto the chair or the bed. Feel the difference in the muscles as they relax. Feel the release from tension, the sense of comfort, the warmth and heaviness of relaxation. [Relax for twenty seconds.]

(4)   Now build up the tension in the upper legs by pulling the knees together and lifting the legs off the bed or chair. Focus on the tightness through the upper legs. Feel the pulling sensations from the hip down and notice the tension in the legs. Focus on that part of your body [ten seconds]. Now release the tension, and let the legs drop heavily down on to the chair or bed. Let the tension disappear. Focus on the feeling of relaxation. Feel the difference in your legs. Focus on the sense of comfort [twenty seconds.]

(5)   Now build up the tension in your stomach by pulling your stomach in towards the spine, very tight. Feel the tension. Feel the tightness and focus on that part of your body [ten seconds]. Now let the stomach go — let it go further and further. Feel the sense of warmth circulating across your stomach. Feel the comfort of relaxation. [For twenty seconds focus on that part of your body].

(6)   Now build up the tension around your chest by taking in a deep breath and holding it. Your chest is expanded, and the muscles are stretched around your chest - feel the tension around your front and your back. Hold your breath [ten seconds]. Now slowly let the air escape and resume normal breathing, letting the air flow in and out smoothly and easily. Feel the difference as the muscles relax in comparison to the tension.

(7)   Moving up to the shoulders, imagine your shoulders are on strings being pulled up towards your ears. Feel the tension around your shoulders, radiating down into your back and up into your neck and the back of your head. Focus on that part of your body. Describe the sensations to yourself. Focus [ten seconds] and then let the shoulders droop down. Let them droop further and further, feeling very relaxed. Feel the sense of relaxation in that part of your body. Focus on the comfort of relaxation [twenty seconds].

(8)   Build up the tension around your neck by pressing the back of your neck towards the chair or bed and pulling your chin down towards your chest. Feel the tightness around the back of the neck spreading up into your head. Focus on the tension [ten seconds]. And, now release, letting your head rest heavily against the bed or chair. Nothing is holding it up except for the support behind. Focus on the relaxation [twenty seconds] and feel the difference from the tension.

(9)   Build up the tension around your mouth and jaw and throat by clenching your teeth and forcing the corners of your mouth back into a forced smile. Hold the tension [ten

seconds]. Feel the tightness in that part of your body. Describe the sensations to yourself. And now release the tension letting the mouth drop down and the muscles around the throat and jaw relax. Focus on the difference in the sensations in that part of your body [twenty seconds.]

(10)   Now build up the tension around your eyes by squeezing your eyes tightly together for a few seconds and release. Let the tension disappear from around your eyes. Feel the difference as the muscles relax.

(11)   Now build up the tension across the lower forehead by frowning, pulling your eyebrows down and towards the center. Feel the tension across your forehead and the top of your head. Focus on the tension [ten seconds] and then release, smoothing out the wrinkles and letting the forehead relax. Feel the difference in the sensations.

(12)   Finally, build up the tension in the upper forehead by raising your eyebrows up as high as you can. Feel the wrinkling and the pulling sensations across the forehead and the top of the head. Hold the tension [ten seconds] and then relax, letting the eyebrows rest down and the tension from your forehead leave. Focus on the sensation of relaxation. Feel the difference in comparison to the tension.

Now your whole body is feeling relaxed and comfortable. As I count from one to five, feel yourself becoming even more relaxed, even further relaxed. One, letting all the tension leave your body. Two, sinking further and further into relaxation. Three, feeling more and more relaxed. Four, feeling very relaxed. Five, deeply relaxed. Now, as you spend a few minutes in this relaxed state, think about your breathing. Feel the cool air as you breathe in and the warm air as you breathe out. Your breathing is slow and regular. And, every time you breathe out, think to yourself the word relax... relax... relax... Feeling comfortable and relaxed... Now, as I count backwards from five to one gradually feel yourself becoming more alert and awake. Five, feeling more awake. Four, coming out of the relaxation. Three, feeling more alert. Two, open your eyes. One, sitting up."

STOP recording for the tape here. Once you learn to do this procedure very effectively, you might lower your heart rate and blood pressure while relaxing. For that reason, it is a good idea not to stand up very quickly after relaxing. Now, practice the exercise.

Assess your experience. Were there any particular parts of your body that were very difficult to relax? Are there any parts of your body where you feel a lot of tension? For very tense areas, it helps to tense and release several times. Were you able to focus your attention on the relaxation? If other thoughts came into your mind, did you let them pass through? Did you feel more relaxed after the exercise? Did you feel any anxiety during the procedure? Repeated practice will enable you to go through the whole procedure without feeling anxious. Be aware that some anxiety may be present initially if you are very sensitive to the sensations that are produced by relaxation. However, rather than that being evidence for you not to do relaxation, it is in fact evidence for you to repeat the relaxation procedure.

Keep a record of every time you practice so that you can observe over time how well you do

5-12

TABLE 5:3

RELAXATION RECORD

Rate concentration and breathing on 0 to 8 point scales

DATE	PRACTICE	RELAXATION AT THE END OF THE EXERCISE	CONCENTRATION DURING THE EXERCISE
	1		
	2		
	1		
	2		
	1		
	2		
	1		
	2		
	1		
	2		
	1		
	2		
	1		
	2		

"Listen . . . You've got to relax . . . The more you think about changing colors, the less chance you'll succeed . . . Shall we try the green background again?"

with the relaxation and any problems that you encounter. This will provide a very good source of feedback for you. Make copies of the RELAXATION RECORD form on Page 5-12. On that form, keep a record of your levels of relaxation and concentration. As mentioned before, the exercise should be practiced two times a day for the next seven days.

If at the end of seven days you are able to complete the 16 muscle group procedure without feeling anxious and with a significant feeling of relaxation (at least 4 on the 0 to 8 point scale), it will be time to practice the 8 muscle group procedure. If you are still experiencing difficulty relaxing, continue with the full 16 muscle group procedure for an additional week. The eight muscle group procedure is the same as the 16 muscle group except that some muscle groups are excluded because of the effects of generalization. That is, by relaxing major areas of your body, other areas will also become relaxed. The muscle groups that we suggest for the eight muscle procedure are as follows: the arm as one unit (upper and lower), the leg as one unit (upper and lower), the stomach, the chest, the shoulders, the neck, the eyes, and the forehead. However, if you find that there is one particular part of your body that becomes very tense, such as your jaw, then you might include that in the procedure. In order to do the arms as one unit, simply tense the lower arm and the upper arms at the same time. Similarly for the legs. Use the same procedure, focusing your attention on the tension feelings and the relaxation feelings, progressing from one muscle group to the other. Then count from 1 to 5 and become more relaxed, and then gradually come out of the relaxation while counting backwards from 5 to 1. Practice the eight muscle procedure two times a day for seven days and keep a record of your practices as before on the RELAXATION RECORD form. Monitoring will provide feedback on your progress for yourself and anyone you're working with. An outline of the relaxation procedures is provided in Table 5:4.

Exercises

1. Breathing Retaining - practice the breathing retraining exercise two times a day, ten minutes each time, for seven days. Keep a record of your practices on the BREATHING RETRAINING RECORD form. Continue to monitor your panics and anxiety using the methods described previously.

2. Relaxation Training - practice the relaxation exercise 2 times a day, for 7 days, proceeding from 16 muscle groups to 8 muscle groups when you feel comfortable and relaxed using the 16 muscle groups. Monitor your practice on the RELAXATION RECORD form. Continue to monitor your anxiety and panic using the methods described earlier.

TABLE 5:4

OUTLINE FOR RELAXATION

1. Quiet location, comfortable chair or bed.

2. Loosen tight clothing.

3. Tense for 10 seconds and relax for 20 seconds the following major muscle groups:

1, 2	lower arms
3, 4	upper arms
5, 6	lower legs
7, 8	upper legs
9	abdomen
10	chest
11	shoulders
12	neck
13	mouth, throat, and jaw
14	eyes
15	lower forehead
16	upper forehead

4. Focus attention on sensations of tension and relaxation.

5. Count 1 to 5 to deepen relaxation, breathe slowly for 2 minutes and count 5 to 1 to become more alert.

6. Practice 2 times per day, for 7 days.

7. Monitor your practice.

8. Proceed to eight muscle-group relaxation when able to relax using 16 muscle group procedure.

1	upper and lower arms
2	upper and lower legs
3	abdomen
4	chest
5	shoulders
6	neck
7	eyes
8	forehead

Answer each question by circling true (T) or false (F). Answers are on page A-2 - A-3.

1.   Overbreathing

     a)   Overbreathing means breathing too much and too
          deeply for the body's needs at a particular
          point in time.   T   F

     b)   Continuous overbreathing is potentially dangerous.   T   F

     c)   When practicing breathing retraining exercises,
          one should focus on completely unrelated material.   T   F

     d)   Speeding up of the breathing rate during the exercise
          is an indication to stop using breathing exercises.   T   F

     e)   The goals of breathing retraining are to reduce
          the symptoms that may begin the panic reaction
          and to reduce overbreathing that may occur during
          panic and during general anxiety.   T   F

2.   Muscular Tension

     a)   Being physically tense all of the time means that
          you will never be able to relax.   T   F

     b)   A lot of muscle tension feeds into cycles of
          anxious anticipation and fear.   T   F

     c)   Symptoms such as fatigue, muscle aches and pains
          and weakness are often related to a high level of
          muscle tension.   T   F

     d)   When doing relaxation exercises, one should try
          to attain complete relaxation in one initial step.   T   F

     e)   The goals of relaxation training are to reduce
          symptoms that may begin the panic reaction and to
          reduce tension that occurs during panic and general
          anxiety.   T   F

CHAPTER 6

Development of Control of Physical Responses

Review

Review your DAILY MOOD and PANIC ATTACK RECORDS over the last week and add the average anxiety and number of panics to your PROGRESS RECORD. Did you notice any other patterns occurring during the week? Were you able to objectively analyze processes involved when you did become fearful: did you look for cues to your panic and did you examine interactions among things you may have said to yourself and different feelings and sensations that you experienced? Now review your monitoring of practices for either the breathing retraining and/or the relaxation. For those who are working with the breathing retraining, focus on the next section of this chapter. For those who are working with relaxation, skip over to the latter section of the chapter.

Breathing Retraining

Did you feel as if you were getting enough air into the diaphragm? Remember, if you feel that you are not getting enough air, push the stomach out a fraction before inhaling. Are you getting symptoms of anxiety when you practice? This is probably due to breathing a little fast or becoming sensitive to breathing patterns when you think about them. Keep practicing and the anxiety will diminish. Are you having trouble concentrating on the counting? Practice will help your concentration, but if you continue to experience difficulty concentrating, it may be helpful to make an audiocassette for yourself on which you record counting at an appropriate rate. Examine your ratings from the BREATHING RETRAINING RECORD for the week. Did the ease with which you could breathe "properly" improve? If not, think about some of the reasons that were suggested earlier and try to make changes based on those possibilities. Keep practicing because it will get easier.

In the last chapter the aim was for you to match your counting with your breathing; i.e., to count when inhaling. From now on, in order to begin to slow down the breathing rate, begin to match your breathing to your counting. That is, count the number and then inhale, think the word "relax" and then exhale. Gradually begin to slow your counting day by day until you can breathe at a rate of around 10 breaths per minute at rest. This means about three seconds in and three seconds out. Continue to practice with one hand on your stomach and one hand on your chest in order to ensure that you are breathing from the diaphragm. Try that procedure now of counting "one" - then breathe in, "relax" - breathe out. "Two" - then breathe in, "relax" - then breathe out, etc. Continue to practice this procedure at least two times a day, monitoring your breathing and concentration with each practice, using the BREATHING RETRAINING RECORD. Practice for the next seven days, gradually slowing the rate of breathing to 10 breaths per minute.

Relaxation

Examining your RELAXATION RECORD for the week, did your levels of relaxation and concentration increase the more you practiced the exercises? Did you have any problems concentrating? If that was the case, just remind yourself to bring your attention back everytime you notice yourself wandering. Were you able to feel relaxation in different parts of your body? If you have certain muscle groups which are difficult to relax, try to practice tensing and releasing them several times. Did you feel under too much pressure to do the relaxation — in other words, had you not devoted enough time for the relaxation and nothing else? These kind of practices must be given priority in order to benefit from them. The amount you get out of these programs is definitely a function of how much effort you put in.

If you feel comfortable doing the eight muscle group procedure and your rating of relaxation is at least four, it is time to break the exercise down to four muscle groups. If, on the other hand, you are still experiencing some problems attaining relaxation, continue with the 16 or eight muscle group procedures for another week. For the four muscle groups, the muscles that we suggest tensing and releasing include the following: stomach, chest, shoulders, and the face as one unit (tense and relax all of your face muscles at one time). Again, if there are different parts of your body which you know are very tense and become a major focus of your attention, you might continue to include the related muscle groups. Use the exact same procedure as described earlier, and practice two times a day for the next seven days. Continue to practice in a relaxing environment and to monitor your levels of concentration and relaxation with each practice using the RELAXATION RECORD form.

Exercise

Practice your breathing or relaxation exercises two times a day over the next seven days, continuing to monitor your practices using the BREATHING RETRAINING or RELAXATION RECORD forms. Continue to use your DAILY MOOD and PANIC ATTACK RECORDS, with special reference to the role of breathing patterns and/or muscle tension in the onset or occurrence of your fearful reactions and generalized anxiety.

Self-Assessment

Answer the following by circling true (T) or false (F). Answers are on page A-3.

1. Skipping out on practices once in a while is okay.   T   F

2. Attention during the exercises is very important.   T   F

3. If it hasn't become any easier by now, then it
    is never going to work.   T   F

4. The monitoring of relaxation and/or breathing
    is necessary because it allows evaluation of progress
    and an objective understanding of how the techniques
    are being applied and their effectiveness.
    It is one part of learning control.   T   F

CHAPTER 7

Refinement of Physical Response Control Techniques and An Introduction to Self-Statement Analysis

Review

Review your DAILY MOOD and PANIC ATTACK RECORDS from the preceding week. Add your information to your PROGRESS RECORD. Spend a few minutes thinking about any patterns that emerged or responses that were different. Did you examine each panic or anxiety episode in terms of a sequential analysis of the original cue and the spiral effect due to the interaction among different aspects of your thoughts, feelings and behaviors?

Breathing Retraining

Now that you are able to breathe at a slower and more comfortable rate, it is time to begin to practice the breathing retraining exercise in different environments. Do it when you are at work, watching TV, at a social event, or wherever you are. Do as many mini-practices as you can during the day. In addition, begin to use the exercise when you become aware of feeling out of breath or a shortness of breath or feeling anxious. At those times, go through the procedure of counting 1 to 10 and back down to 1, slowing the breathing rate to 3 or more seconds in and 3 or more seconds out. Concentrate on the breathing as you practice. In other words, apply the control that you have learned to real situations. If it doesn't work at first, that is okay; just continue to apply the strategy, and after each time you have used the technique, evaluate objectively how well it worked and if you could have done something differently. Don't give up if it doesn't work right away because learning is a gradual process. Also, remember that even if you don't immediately control the symptoms of breathlessness, you are not in danger.

Relaxation Training

Now that you have been able to relax using four muscle groups, it is time to introduce what is called recall and cue-controlled relaxation. Instead of tensing up the muscles first, now try to relax each of those four major muscle groups by remembering or recalling the feelings of relaxation that you have experienced during your prior exercises. Focus on a particular muscle group and think about relaxing. Think about the sensations of relaxation such as heaviness, warmth, or a floating feeling. Progressively focus on each part of your body [for 20 seconds each time] and then count one to five to achieve a deeper state of relaxation. Focus on slow, relaxed breathing for one to two minutes. Then count back from five to one. Gradually become more alert as you count back to one. This may take more practice than the other exercises, as it requires intense concentration on your body and becoming relaxed. As you try to recall the relaxation, describe as clearly as you can in your own mind the feeling of relaxation in the relevant part of your body. Also, physically let go the tension if it is present by doing things such as drooping your shoulders down or letting your stomach relax outwards. As you focus on becoming relaxed, continue to think to yourself the word "relax." Repeat "relax" over and over again so that it develops, by power of association, a meaning. Later we will be using that word as a signal for relaxation in the same way as various sensations have become a signal for you to feel fearful.

Practice the recall procedure two times a day for the next seven days or until you are able to relax by recall easily (i.e., can achieve a relaxation rating of at least four). Once you are able to do that, continue on to the next step.

The next step is called cue-relaxation, and it relies on the word "relax". Think of the word "relax" and as you think of that word, attempt to review your body and let go all of the tension. Try it now. Again, this might take more practice than earlier techniques because of the intense concentration. Try to practice it as often as you can, at any time that you have a few seconds to relax. In addition, try to relax in different places such as when you are driving a car, waiting at a stoplight, when you are walking down the street, when you are in a conversation with someone, wherever you are so that it becomes a skill that you can apply when necessary. Apply cue-relaxation whenever you notice any physical tension in your body. In addition, apply it when you feel yourself become anxious or panicky. Use it as a control technique to gain mastery over your emotions. An important part of why the relaxation method is effective is because relaxing interferes with the action tendency to want to escape or run. In a sense, it is the opposite action tendency of staying where you are and relaxing. So it is very important that you begin to introduce relaxation whenever you feel agitation building up. It is a competing response. It may take time before you become very successful at applying the relaxation response because the tendency to want to run or escape has been reinforced in the past. However, do not be frustrated if it does not work at first, just continue to practice.

Beginnings of Self-Statement Analysis

We discussed in earlier chapters the importance of misinterpretations and gave a lot of corrective information for you to integrate into your understanding of what is panic and anxiety. However, now it is time to introduce more direct techniques for modifying the kinds of information and thoughts or statements that you say to yourself, especially those that occur at times when you are feeling the emotions of anxiety or fear. It is possible that the corrective information given earlier has changed your overall perspective but that you have found that it does not work as well at times when you are feeling very anxious or panicky. For example, you might think that "when I am calm and relaxed, I can say that there is no chance that I will collapse when I have my next panic, but when I am feeling panicky, I really feel like I am going to collapse." That is the connection that occurs between emotions and thoughts, just as when we are depressed, it is much easier to think about very sad memories than when we are happy. However, this is not a reason to assume that it is not possible to change your reactions. Modifying or correcting what you tell yourself is in effect changing the structure of panic. By changing your self-statements you will eliminate a big part of the panic reaction and, therefore, reduce the frequency of panic attacks.

You might also be saying that, "I don't tell myself anything when I panic, it just comes out of the blue." As mentioned earlier, there is definitely a dimension of conscious awareness of thought processes. That is, sometimes you may be strongly aware of yourself thinking very frightening things (e.g. really believing that you are in danger) and at other times the information you are giving yourself may be very automatized so that you are not even aware of its influence. Two experts on this topic, Aaron T. Beck and Gary Emery have termed this quality as automaticity and discreteness in cognitions. The term automatic means that the thoughts occur very rapidly and may be outside of the person's direct awareness. The term discrete refers to the fact that these thoughts are very specific in content and may vary across situations. The focus of your worry may differ from one situation to another; you may be mostly afraid of embarrassment in one situation and mostly afraid of being alone and in danger in another situation. The implication is that sometimes you have to search very hard for the particular thoughts that are present, and it is important to pursue the thoughts until you identify a very specific prediction that is being made. Identifying the thought as "I felt terrible" is too global and may serve only to increase your anxiety about a particular experience by virtue of being so global and nondirective. Ask yourself for further analysis. What do you picture happening? What do you think could happen as a result of feeling terrible?

Go back to each episode of anxiety and panic that you have monitored over the last couple of weeks. What were the major kinds of thoughts going through your mind just before, during and after the episodes of anxiety and panic? Are your descriptions very general, such as "I felt horrible" or "I felt anxious." If so, try to remember the event as it occurred and try to think of what you said to yourself or thought at that time. Why was it so terrible? What did you think could happen? What do you think would happen if you panicked in the particular situation? What would it mean if you felt like you were going to lose control?

Examples would be something like this: "I was afraid that if I went into the store, I would feel very anxious, start to look for a way out, and then panic and not know how to get out. I would feel like I would have to get out because if I stayed in that store and panicked, I could really lose control. Losing control would mean that I would become overwhelmed by the feeling of anxiety and I couldn't stand it. Being overwhelmed means that the feelings could get really intense and I would be afraid that I would explode or go crazy because the feelings are so intense. I have an image of people gathering around me, trying to restrain me, and then being taken away by the police."

Once this level of specificity in thought identification is achieved, it is much more open to direct challenging. Stopping at the point of "I am afraid" does not allow introduction of specific techniques for changing the way you think. Therefore, it is very important to pursue the thought as far as you can by continuing to question it. If you don't question it you can't reduce your anxiety and panic.

Remember Jill, who we introduced in earlier chapters. When she first attended our clinic, Jill was very sensitive to fluctuations in her heart rate. Her first statements were "It's just a horrible feeling - and I can get so afraid that I become totally out of control." In this statement, Jill used two very global descriptions - that the feeling is horrible and that she totally loses control. The following is an illustration of how the therapist helped Jill to become aware of the bases for her descriptions.

Therapist: "What do you mean exactly when you say that the feeling of a
                racing heart is horrible? What is horrible about it?"

Client: "Well, it makes me feel very scared."

Therapist: "What are you scared of?"

Client: "It makes me worry about something going wrong - physically."

Therapist: "What do you think could happen?"

Client: "Maybe, no, I definitely feel - that my heart will just keep going faster and faster and eventually it will stop."

Therapist: "And then what?"

Client: "Well, then I'll die"

Therapist: "So actually your statement that the feeling of a racing heart is horrible is based on images of terrible things happening for which you have no real evidence."

Client: "Well, yes. I guess so. I never thought of it like that."

Therapist: "What about the description of totally losing control?
What do you mean by that?"

Client: "That's hard to describe. I guess I don't really know what it means. I just feel out of control."

Therapist: "Well, what do you think could happen if you were totally out of control?"

Client: "That I couldn't stop the way I was feeling."

Therapist: "And what would happen if you couldn't stop the feeling?"

Client: "Well, the feeling would get so intense that I wouldn't be able to function any more. I'd just be a wreck."

Therapist: "And then what?"

Client: "Well, that would be the end of my life. I'd spend the rest of my life doing nothing."

Therapist: "So again, the statement of losing control is based on some quite specific predictions you are making. And, really, those predictions are ones for which you have no bases."

As you can see, when pursued, the nature of Jill's thoughts became clearer and from that point on it was easy to dispell her fears about losing control or being horrified by minor heart rate fluctuations.

Probability Overestimation

There seem to be two general types of "errors" in thoughts or self-statements that are important to anxiety and panic. The first one is identified as probability overestimation. Can you think of any times recently when you caught yourself jumping to a negative conclusion which resulted in anxiety or fear and which you later found out to be an incorrect interpretation or an incorrect prediction?

Think of examples that are relevant to both general anxiety and to panic fear. A typical example of overestimation in the case of general anxiety is "nothing will get done on time" and a typical example in the case of panic fear is "I will faint." Go back through all the panics of which you have kept records over the last few weeks. Try to remember what thoughts you had for each of those panics. Now ask yourself if any of the events you feared happening actually occurred. What does the result tell you?

"The fuel light's on, Frank! We're all going to die! ... Wait, wait. ... Oh, my mistake—that's the intercom light."

You might say "yes, I know those things are not going to happen but I still get frightened by the possibility." Why is it that overestimation errors occur repeatedly despite disconfirmation? Why does one continue to be afraid of going crazy or continue to be afraid of passing out, despite the fact that panic has occurred hundreds of times without ever going crazy or passing out? There are several reasons, such as believing that it "could still happen." Also, believing with relief when the event is over that "I was lucky that time" instead of realizing the inaccuracy of the original prediction is another reason for the continuation of the overestimations. A common example would be "if I had not gone to the emergency room, I don't know what would have happened." In other words, real evidence is ignored or distorted to fit into the bias of interpreting that there is or was a danger present. Many times we have heard clients say such things as "it would have been terrible if I hadn't found my husband" or "I know I was really on the edge of totally losing it" or "I don't know how I survived through it, I'm sure I wouldn't be able to go through another one like that." All of these statements are based on very biased interpretations. The truth is that the panic episodes were survived because there was no real danger.

Another reason why the overestimations continue despite repeated disconfirmation is simply that, due to the pattern of associations that have built up over time, it is likely that catastrophizing or overestimating thoughts will come into your mind when you are feeling anxious despite your logical understanding at other times that they are not accurate. However, that does not mean that they should not be subjected to a logical analysis of their accuracy. That is, just because a thought comes into your mind doesn't mean that it is any more accurate than if it never came to your mind. In some cases, the presence of the thought can elicit more anxiety and panic, but worrying about losing control does not mean you will lose control and worrying about dying does not mean you will die. Instead of treating those thoughts as reasons to become more frightened, evaluate them objectively.

Examine some of your predictions and determine whether they are examples of overestimation. Use your predictions from past and future events. For past events, if you tell yourself that unless you had called someone or managed to get out of the situation when you panicked, you would not have survived, then you are most likely overestimating the danger you were in. For future events, are you predicting that the next time you panic you <u>could</u> <u>really</u> lose control? In Jill's case, as soon as she became aware that the reason she was afraid of losing control was because she predicted that the feelings of panic would never stop, she then realized that her prediction was inaccurate, because indeed her panic attacks, like everyone else's, were very brief.

You may conduct the same kind of analysis with general anxiety. For example, an overestimation of a past event might be "my boss was probably very angry with me last week when he did not smile during our conversation" and an example of a future overestimation might be "I got through it this time, but next time I have people over for dinner, I'm sure that everything will result in a failure."

The basis of the method for changing or challenging these overestimations is to question the evidence for your probability judgments. Remember to treat thoughts as <u>hypotheses</u> or <u>guesses</u> rather than as fact and that before you make a judgment, you should examine the evidence for your prediction. Your interpretations of any given object or event represent one of many possible interpretations. The kind of interpretation that you give may be very different from someone else's. So, it is important to explore alternatives. This is especially important given the knowledge that in anxious states we tend to be biased in our interpretations. Think of your anxiety on a dimension with neutral or no anxiety at the mid-point, extreme anxiety at one end and extreme calmness at the other. If you view an impending situation with dread due to the prediction that something bad might happen, your emotion is obviously going to be charged towards the extreme anxiety end. In contrast, if you view the same situation with a carefree, "no matter what happens" attitude, your emotion will be charged towards the calmness or relaxation end. In other words, you have the ability to create an emotional state in either direction. Obviously, the goal is not to remove anxiety concerning real threats but to minimize your anxious bias in situations in which there is no real threat.

In order to evaluate the evidence for a prediction, ask yourself what are the real odds of this happening, has this ever happened before, what is the evidence that it will or will not happen? This requires you to consider all of the facts and all of the evidence before you make a prediction of the likelihood of something happening. For example, you may assume that you are going to fail a test or do poorly in an exam or presentation and overlook the fact that you have prepared very carefully for the exam or presentation. Or, a friend may be acting in a hostile or cold manner and you may assume that they are displeased with you and overlook the fact that they may be feeling angry at someone else or that they have had a bad day. In terms of panic, you may assume that feeling tingling in the left arm is a sign of a heart attack and overlook the fact that you are in good health and that you have experienced the tingling many times before without suffering a heart attack. Certainly, Jill was overlooking the fact that none of her panic attacks had ever continued forever. It is possible that you are making negative predictions on the basis of a very limited set of past examples. For example, you may predict that you will fail an exam or become anxious because you have done poorly on similar exams or have become anxious in similar situations before. However, you may be overlooking many instances in which you have done well on such exams or were not anxious in those situations. You may in fact be confusing low probabilities with high probabilities or acting and feeling as if negative outcomes are certainties rather than possibilities. Unrealistic statements which turn possibilities into certainties and create anxiety are "I know I am going to panic the next time I go into the mall" and "I know I am going to have an accident at some time in the near future."

Take your own examples of overestimations and examine the evidence for each prediction. The very fact that you ask yourself for evidence means that you interrupt the emotional cycle and prevent yourself from being "carried along" or controlled by the fear. Become an objective observer. To help you do this, make a list on one side of a page of examples of your own overestimations and provide corrective evidence for each example. A list of examples is provided in Table 7:1.

Table 7:1

MODIFYING SELF-STATEMENTS

I - Overestimating

OVERESTIMATION ERRORS	THE EVIDENCE
1. I could faint the next time I panic.	What are the real chances of fainting? What is the probability on a 0-100 point scale? Have I ever fainted before?
2. I could have a car accident when I feel dizzy while driving.	What evidence do I have? How many times have I felt dizzy when driving and how many times have I had a car accident when feeling dizzy.
3. If I'm left alone, I'll really lose it and go crazy.	What has happened in the past when I've been alone? Or, have I ever tested out my prediction to see what would happen if I was alone? I might feel anxious but what evidence do I have that I would go crazy?
4. The pains in my chest must mean that I'm having a heart attack.	What is the evidence against this possibility? What were the results from my last medical check-up? How many times have I felt the pain before? Have I ever had a heart attack?

Exercise

In addition to continuing to apply breathing retraining and/or relaxation throughout the day at anytime when you feel anxious, pay special attention to errors of overestimation in your thoughts. (You no longer need to monitor your practice of the breathing or relaxation exercise.) If episodes of panic or anxiety have not occurred recently or are not occurring currently, think about past anxious/panicky times and identify what kind of thoughts were going through your mind and how they could be subjected to a more evidence-based analysis. Continue to use your DAILY MOOD and PANIC ATTACK RECORDS.

Self-Assessment

Answer each of the following by circling true (T) or false (F). Answers are on page A-3 - A-4.

1. Thoughts have no impact on how one feels.   T   F

2. Part of changing one's thoughts or self-statements
    involves being very specific in the description of
    thoughts.   T   F

3. This kind of analysis doesn't work because what I
    am afraid of could still happen.   T   F

4. Questioning what one thinks interrupts the emotional
    cycle and allows one to gain control.   T   F

CHAPTER 8

Continuation of Self Statement Analysis
Manipulating Your Own Mind

Review

Review your DAILY MOOD and PANIC ATTACK RECORDS from the preceding week. Add your data (average anxiety and number of panics) to your PROGRESS RECORD. Spend a few minutes thinking about any patterns that have emerged or responses that were different from the preceding weeks. Did you examine each panic and anxiety episode within the framework of a sequential analysis of the beginning cue, the spiraling due to the interaction among different responses (physical, behavioral and thoughts) and the consequence? Were you a successful, objective observer of your own responses? It is extremely important that you continue this approach.

Breathing Retraining

Were you able to apply the breathing retraining technique during the preceding week at times when you noticed yourself feeling out of breath or anxious? What was the effect of applying the breathing method? Did you attempt to apply this strategy with a sense of desperation as a method of escaping or preventing at all costs the symptoms of anxiety? If so, you should reevaluate the purpose of applying this strategy. Breathing retraining is not designed as a technique to prevent a terrible event from happening (i.e., panic). Rather, it is a technique designed to change one of the components that is central to the emotional states of anxiety and panic, which is, of course, the physical component. It is important that you use the strategy in that perspective rather than as a method of escaping or avoiding some future event. If you are using breathing retraining with des-peration, you are in fact adding fuel to the fire that creates further tension and anxiety. You are trying to fight off an event and by fighting you are adding to the intensity. Were you able to pick up on early signals suggesting the importance of reestablishing slower and deeper breathing patterns, or was it not until you found yourself gasping for breath that you applied the technique? If the latter was the case, attempt to become more aware of the earlier signs that can prompt you to exercise breathing control (again, not as a method of preventing a catastrophe, but as the more effective application of a technique designed to reduce the somatic symptoms). Remember, even if the physical symptoms are not immediately alleviated, you are not in danger. Continue to apply the breathing strategy when-ever you notice yourself becoming anxious or feeling short of breath until it becomes a very natural response and replaces your prior response of overbreathing.

Relaxation Training

Were you able to apply relaxation, using the cue-controlled format, at times when you noticed yourself feeling tense, anxious or panicky over the preceding week? Were you able to discriminate levels of tension in your body and apply relaxation as a technique upon first noticing the build up of tension? Or, did you wait until you became extremely tense and rigid before applying the strategy? If the latter was the case, attempt to become more aware of the earlier signs of tension that can prompt you to apply relaxation. However, this should not be confused as an attempt to prevent at all costs the experience of anxiety or panic. Did you use relaxation as a method of escaping a catastrophe? Remember, relaxation is not intended as an escape or avoidance strategy, which is used in states of desperation, but rather it is intended as a technique that reduces one of the components which contributes to the anxiety and panic spirals. Continue to use the relaxation as a strategy over the following week at times when you notice yourself feeling anxious, frightened, or tense.

Catastrophic Thinking

Did you pay attention to your thinking patterns over the preceding week and notice times when you were overestimating the likelihood of particular events? Did you attempt to challenge that error by questioning the evidence? Don't be discouraged if such questioning seems artificial at first, or does not immediately result in feeling less anxious/panicky. As with the somatic exercises, thinking exercises require practice, because you are learning to replace an old habit of responding with a new one.

The second type of "error" in the way that information is processed when feeling anxious or frightened is called catastrophic thinking. That is, in addition to being frightened by the occurrence of an event that is actually unlikely to happen (overestimation) unnecessary anxiety and fear often arises from viewing an event as "dangerous", "insufferable" or "catastrophic" when in actuality it is not. Typical kinds of catastrophic thoughts are: "If other people noticed that I was feeling very anxious or panicky, it would be terrible and I could never face them again"; "It would be disastrous if I fainted"; "If everything is not perfect when my friends visit, I will be a failure." The point is that when thinking like this, we understandably respond with increased anxiety and fear, without every stopping to examine the validity of those kinds of statements. If you stop to examine the actual event realistically, it is usually the case that it is not as catastrophic as first thought. For example, if one fainted from acute hyperventilation, it is not such a terrible event because fainting is actually an adaptive mechanism designed to reestablish a balance or a homeostasis in the body and the worst that can happen is a brief feeling of disorientation after regaining consciousness.

Think about the worst things you envision happening when you are feeling very anxious or panicky. Review the episodes of anxiety and panic that you have recorded over the past two weeks and determine whether any of the thoughts associated with those occurrences were catastrophic. It helps if you distinguish the feelings from the actual thought. That is, it is highly likely that you felt as if it were terrible and you felt that you wouldn't be able to survive, but the thought that you would not survive or that the event would be terrible is catastrophic. Think of times when you have said to yourself "that would be terrible" or "I couldn't stand it", or, in reference to the future, "I couldn't stand to live through that again." Similarly, a statement such as "I am so frightened that I might slip back into the way I felt several months ago when I was panicking more frequently — I couldn't stand to go through that again" is very catastrophic. Obviously, if that is the kind of information you give to yourself, it is only natural that you continue to be very distressed. One client who attended our clinic was initially very anxious because she believed that she would not be able to cope mentally or physically with any more panic attacks - that the BIG one was going to, in a sense, destroy her. Therefore, she was constantly anxious and on guard for the next attack. Instead of trying to understand what panic attacks really are, and instead of realizing that she had coped with all of her previous panic attacks, she focused on not being able to survive.

Another common statement is "Anything could happen the next time I panic and that is what frightens me. I don't know what it is but it is going to be something bad." Again, this kind of statement is generating anxiety by believing and feeling as if there is a real threat but if you examine the evidence and consider the worst that can happen, it is not as catastrophic as you first think. As mentioned before, remember to pull apart the emotion and the thought. It may <u>feel</u> bad, but part of that feeling is based on a catastrophic thought process. Another example of catastrophic thinking in relation to more general anxiety is "I felt as if I was on the verge of a nervous breakdown and could not cope with anything or anyone when I had to deal with all those pressures at work last summer", or "I'll drop out of school and be a failure for the rest of my life if I don't pass the exam." Can you classify any of your own statements into the category of catastrophic thinking?

The method of directly challenging these kinds of statements is to first gather basic information about the possibility of real threat or danger and then critically evaluate the actual severity. Decatastrophizing involves imagining the consequences of the worst actually happening and then evaluating the severity of those consequences. This kind of analysis can be conducted with events that are both likely to happen (e.g., shaking when you feel anxious in a public situation) and unlikely to happen (e.g., fainting when panicking). If the worst that is considered likely to happen is death or loss of significant other or behaviors that you view to be in strong conflict with religious beliefs, then decatastrophizing may not be as effective because in your own mind, it is not appropriate to say that it is not so bad to die or not so bad to lose someone very close to you. Fears of death or loss are generally more appropriate to the analysis of overestimation — that is, how likely is it that you will die the next time you panic, and how likely is it that you will do something totally against your beliefs?

Ask yourself what is the worst possible thing that could happen the next time you panic or what is the worst thing that could happen in an impending situation about which you are worried? What if you actually did faint when you panicked? What if you actually did look very shaky when you were speaking to others? What if you actually did get up and walk out of a room because you felt trapped? Your first reaction to these questions might be something like "that would be awful or terrible", or "I couldn't stand it." However, when you think carefully and critically about these assumptions, you will find that you have prematurely assumed them to to be catastrophic. For example, what would happen if people really did think you looked foolish because you were shaky and sweaty? Does it really matter what these people think? If they are strangers, then why should it matter what they think because you are unlikely to ever see them again. If they are friends, then this particular incident is not going to change their whole opinion of you, so it again doesn't matter. And what if people did think poorly of you, does that mean you will never enjoy life again? In other words, in actuality, you can stand or tolerate or bear any misfortune that happens to you. It is only the statement that creates the anxiety — the statement that you cannot stand it. In its most extreme form, decastrophizing goes so far as pointing out that anybody can stand anything until they die and then there is no reason to stand it anymore. Decatastrophizing can be summed up in one phrase - So what! So what if I faint; so what if I look foolish. Let's take Jill as an example. In Chapter 3, we used her panic attacks to demonstrate the importance of the sequence of events that results in panicky feelings. In one of her examples, Jill described being afraid and embarrassed if she panicked in a restaurant. When asked to specify further what she imagined happening if she panicked in that situation that would make her feel embarrassed, she replied that she would appear so obviously terrified that everyone would know how she felt and would, therefore, think that she was really weird. In addition to helping Jill realize that she was overestimating the probability of others noticing her and of others thinking that she was weird, the therapist helped Jill understand that even if she was upset about others really thinking she was weird, that upset would not last forever.

You may find that as you begin to focus on these kinds of images and thoughts you will experience an increase in anxiety. This is because the thoughts are anxiety provoking, since there may still be an element of disbelief involved on your part that needs to be challenged. In other words, you may still feel deep down that the probability is high that you're going to die. In addition, you may have tried to avoid thinking about those consequences in the past because they frighten you. However, as with any procedure that requires you to confront directly the things of which you are afraid, you will find that the thoughts will become less and less important and less anxiety provoking the more that you face them. Only by facing them directly are you in a position to evaluate whether the consequences that are viewed as terrible or catastrophic would indeed be as intolerable as you believe them to be, and to realize that the anxiety or the embarrassment that you consider to be unbearable is actually going to be **time limited** and **manageable**.

One common thought is that the anxiety and panic are going to continue forever. This reflects both overestimating and catastrophizing because the concept of "continuing forever" implies an inability to cope and a sense of vulnerability. A sense of vulnerability is usually based on overestimating and catastrophic thinking - an important point to remember. Apply this kind of evaluation to the thoughts that you have had over the past couple of weeks in relation to episodes of anxiety and panic. Make a list of your major catastrophic thoughts on one side of a page and respond with decatastrophizing challenges on the other side of the page. A list of examples is shown in Table 8:1.

It is now up to you to apply these strategies anytime you feel anxious or panicky. It would help to review periodically the last two chapters because sometimes the anxious types of thoughts seem stronger when in the midst of feeling anxious. To help you keep on top of anxious-bias in your thinking, use the SELF-STATEMENT RATING FORM shown on page 8-6. Identify the major concern that occurs to you when you are panicky and also the major concern that occurs when you are generally anxious. Once a week, record your estimates of the probability that the event is actually going to happen when you panic and also your estimate of how well you could cope if the event did happen. Do the same for your general anxiety concerns. Rate the probability and coping dimensions on 0-100 point scales where 0 = no chance of it happening and no ability to cope and 100 = definitely will occur and complete ability to cope. Once again, you may wish to remove the rating form from the book and make copies of it. Rate these dimensions in terms of your objective understanding and not in terms of how you feel. Over time, notice the reduction in the estimates of probability and an increase in your estimates of your ability to cope. Both aspects reflect the development of your control over your emotions. For Jill, her most disturbing thought when panicking was that she would be the focus of everyone else's attention and they would think that she was crazy. At first she rated the probability to be quite high and her ability to cope very low. Over time, however, you can see the changes. Similarly, in terms of general anxiety she was very concerned about the health of her child. With time she realized that even if he did become ill, she would be able to cope. Rate your estimates now in the first week row.

Table 8:1

MODIFYING SELF-STATEMENTS

II - Catastrophizing

CATASTROPHIZING (What if . . .)	DECATASTROPHIZING (So what!!)
1. What if I did faint in front of a lot of people - that would be terrible?	If I fainted there would be a reason and my body would be reestablishing a balance. The people around me would not know what was going on. They would try to help. What if they did think I fainted because I was nervous? So what! I'll still survive.
2. What if I was shaking terribly when talking to other people? What if they thought I was crazy?	Do I know these people? If they are strangers, does it matter what they think? If they are friends, no matter what they think at that time we will still be friends. Anyway, I can still live through the embarrassment.
3. What if I'm trapped in the elevator for an hour and panic the whole time? I couldn't cope.	Yes, I might feel anxious for the whole time I'm in there, but what else can happen? So what if I'm anxious!
4. My whole life is terrible; I can't go on. One day I'll just collapse and that will be the end.	Let's say I did reach a point of physical and mental exhaustion and I "collapsed" - meaning, I would become withdrawn and immobile. After some time of recovery I would be back up again. I would survive.

Table 8:2

SELF-STATEMENT RATING FORM

<u>PANIC-FEAR</u>   <u>ANXIETY</u>

Event: _____   Event: _____

Use 0 to 100 point scales where 0 = no probability/no ability to cope and 100 = definitely will occur and complete ability to cope.

	Probability it will occur 0-100	How well I can cope if it does occur 0-100	Probability it will occur 0-100	How well I can cope if it does occur 0-100
1st Week	_____	_____	_____	_____
2nd Week	_____	_____	_____	_____
3rd Week	_____	_____	_____	_____
4th Week	_____	_____	_____	_____
5th Week	_____	_____	_____	_____
6th Week	_____	_____	_____	_____

Table 8:3

<u>Jill's SELF-STATEMENT RATING FORM</u>

<u>PANIC-FEAR</u>   <u>ANXIETY</u>

Event: <u>Others will think I'm crazy</u>   Event: <u>My son will get sick</u>

Use 0 to 100 point scales where 0 = no probability/no ability to cope and 100 = definitely will occur and complete ability to cope.

	Probability it will occur 0-100	How well I can cope if it does occur 0-100	Probability it will occur 0-100	How well I can cope if it does occur 0-100
1st Week	80	10	75	20
2nd Week	70	10	50	30
3rd Week	60	40	50	40
4th Week	40	60	50	45
5th Week	30	70	50	55
6th Week	10	75	50	80

Exercise

Over the next seven days, continue to apply either the breathing retraining exercise or the relaxation exercise in situations where you notice physical symptoms or anxiety. Also, continue to use your DAILY MOOD and PANIC ATTACK RECORDS. In addition, be aware of any errors in your thinking (overestimation or catastrophizing) and apply corrective challenging statements. Specifically, at the end of each day look at your PANIC ATTACK and DAILY MOOD RECORD. For each panic and anxiety episode, go through the following steps.

1. Identify specific thoughts or self-statements before and after.

2. Determine whether these thoughts were overestimations and/or catastrophic.

3. Examine the evidence and/or ask yourself "so what."

It is extremely important that you review your high anxiety and panicky times in this way. By so doing, you will learn to apply these more adaptive styles of thinking when you do feel anxious or fearful. Do not be disheartened if initially, at the time you are feeling very anxious, it is more difficult to apply these modifications to your self-statements. Keep working at it, and it will become easier.

Self-Assessment

Answer each of the following by circling true (T) or false (F). Answers are on page A-4.

1. The fact that I have thoughts about being overwhelmed or collapsing means that these things are actually going to happen.   T   F

2. No one else has these kinds of thoughts. I must be really crazy.   T   F

3. Even if it is difficult to think more rationally when I am feeling very anxious or panicky, I should continue to try to understand what I am saying to myself, how that is adding to the fear, and how to change those statements.   T   F

4. Forcing myself to think about the worst that could happen will make me anxious initially but the more I think about it in an objective way, the less anxious I will feel.   T   F

CHAPTER 9

The Unexpected Becomes Predictable

Review

Review your DAILY MOOD and PANIC ATTACK RECORDS over the preceding week. Add your information (average anxiety and number of panic attacks) to your PROGRESS RECORD. Spend a few minutes thinking about any patterns that emerged or responses that were different. Can you think of each episode of panic and anxiety in an objective way by understanding the sequence of events that preceded, occurred during, and followed the episode? Go to your SELF-STATE-MENT RATING FORM and record your evidence-based probability and coping judgments. Have they changed from last week? If not, try to determine why. Are you ignoring evidence or catastrophizing?

Breathing Retraining and Relaxation Training

Were you able to apply the appropriate strategy at times when you noticed symptoms of anxiety or feelings of anxiety? Did you apply it as a response strategy rather than as a desperation attempt to escape the feelings? Were you able to apply the strategy when you first noticed the symptoms instead of waiting until the symptoms were very intense? Continue to use these techniques whenever they are appropriate - make them a natural part of your behavior.

Self-Statements

At the end of each day and at times when you have felt anxious or panicky, have you been able to identify very specifically the particular thoughts or statements going through your mind? Have you categorized those self-statements as overestimations and/or catastrophic? Were you able to apply appropriate challenging self-statements which correct overestimations and decatastrophize? Were you able to say SO WHAT! Although it might feel artificial and forced initially to continually examine your thoughts and modify them, as you practice more and more, the newer style of thinking will become more natural. Although you might tell yourself now that the likelihood of a imminent heart attack is very slim, you might still feel that it could be a possibility. Keep working with it and your belief will change.

In order to give a boost to your disconfirmation of certain thoughts and, thereby, reduce their likelihood of occurring to you, it is helpful to actually test your predictions. "Prediction testing" is an extension of the principles that have already been established and is based on the realization that our thoughts and interpretations are guesses or hypotheses and are not facts. That is, as mentioned earlier, our interpretations represent one of several possible interpretations of any given event, and they tend to be biased in ways that are dependent on things like mood.

Think of specific anxiety provoking events that could occur over the next week. Make a list of the self-statements that typically occur to you in anticipation of or engagement in those situations, using the PREDICTION TESTING FORM shown below. For example, if you are anticipating a social event, you might identify a typical self-statement as "I am going to feel so anxious that no one will want to speak to me." After you have identified the self-statements for each situation, rate each one on a 0-100 point scale in terms of how likely you think it is that the event will occur, where 0 refers to no chance of it happening, 100 refers to definitely will happen and 50 refers to moderate chance it will happen. Make these particular ratings in reference to how you typically <u>feel</u> when worrying about those events; that is, at this point don't logically evaluate the probability. Just record the number in reference to how you typically feel. Then, put those lists of situations, self-statements and ratings aside for a week. At the end of the week, record whether the events about which you were worried actually did occur. In other words, this is a way of putting into action the method of modifying your thoughts that we have already discussed. It is another way of helping you realize that your thoughts can have a very powerful impact and yet be very inaccurate. Remember that this is not an estimation of how anxious or uncomfortable you would feel in a given situation. For example, a specific self-statement may be "I will be too anxious to understand what John is saying to me." That might be rated with a probability of 50 prior to the event. After the event, when asking yourself whether you actually did understand what was said, you may protest that you did understand but that you felt extremely anxious which made it harder to listen. However, the question is "could you understand" and that is the basis for the rating. Examples of events that Jill anticipated and her ratings of the probability of certain things happening for each event are listed in Table 9:2. When she rated whether her concerns actually eventuated or not at the end of the week, she was very well able to see how much she anticipated without real cause. Therefore, next time she anticipated things like that happening, she was able to challenge her anticipations on the basis of her own evidence.

Looking for Causes of Unexpected Panics

If you still believe that some of your panic attacks are unexpected and, therefore, you continue to be frightened because you don't know when the next one will occur, the following section will be particularly appropriate for you. An analysis of causes involves the detection of all the possible triggers to anxiety and panic. Understanding the specific trigger or precipitants removes anxiety associated with uncertainty and helps to decrease the tendency to search for irrational reasons such as being in serious physical danger. Also, the identification of precipitants helps to develop a sense of personal control by removing the feeling that you are a victim of your emotions.

An important part of this analysis is the awareness that experiencing physical symptoms does not necessarily mean panic or anxiety; everyone experiences different physical symptoms at different times for very natural reasons. In other words, the experience of physical symptoms <u>per se</u> may occur seemingly unpredictably, as a result of fluctuations in hormonal levels or natural biological rhythms. However, the presence of those symptoms or sensations does not mean the presence of panic or anxiety unless you respond to those symptoms with fear or anxiety. Given your sensitivity to panic-related sensations (such as a racing heart or nausea, etc.), it is much more likely that you will notice normal fluctuations that would otherwise pass unnoticed. Then, if you add fear to the cycle, those sensations are likely to intensify. Obviously, the goal of this whole program is to reduce your fear reaction to those sensations which will in turn reduce the intensity of the sensations when they do occur, and reduce your focus of attention upon those sensations.

The second major objective of an analysis of causes is to realize that all panics and anxiety are related to cues. They are <u>reactions</u>. Sometimes the precipitant or cue is very easy to identify, sometimes it is misidentified and at other times, it is more subtle and more difficult to identify. When it is difficult to identify, the panic seems to be unexpected. It is sometimes difficult to be aware of the reasons for which a particular pattern of behavior emerged at any given time without doing a careful analysis. This is true for all forms of behavior, including smoking, eating, and drinking. Although panic is a sudden and intense experience, that does <u>not</u> mean that it is spontaneous or unrelated to prior events.

Table 9:1

PREDICTION TESTING FORM

Upcoming Events	Self-Statements	Probability Based On How I Typically Feel 0-100	After The Event Did It Occur Yes/No
_____	_____	_____	_____
_____	_____		
_____	_____	_____	_____
_____	_____		
_____	_____	_____	_____
_____	_____		
_____	_____	_____	_____
_____	_____		
_____	_____	_____	_____

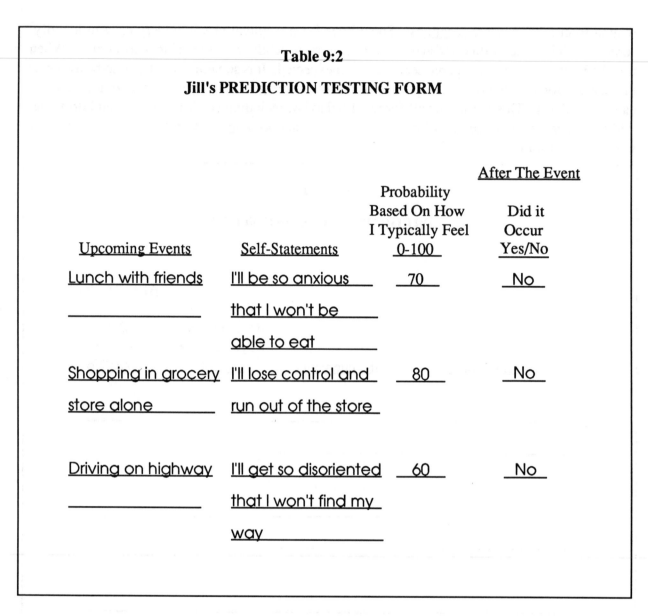

Table 9:2

Jill's PREDICTION TESTING FORM

		Probability Based On How I Typically Feel 0-100	After The Event Did it Occur Yes/No
Upcoming Events	Self-Statements		
Lunch with friends	I'll be so anxious that I won't be able to eat	70	No
Shopping in grocery store alone	I'll lose control and run out of the store	80	No
Driving on highway	I'll get so disoriented that I won't find my way	60	No

There are two good examples of what seems initially to be unexpected panic but, in fact, is very likely related to subtle cues. One is the experience of feeling very relaxed at home and then panicking. A second is waking from sleep in a state of panic.

It is very normal to have wide ranging fluctuations in physiological rhythms during the night. However, in the case of a person who is very sensitive to and frightened by different somatic sensations, it is possible that relatively normal fluctuations that occur during the night may awaken the person who then panics almost immediately because of the awareness of these sensations while in a state of disorientation. It is also possible, although not yet proven, that certain patterns of breathing may be implicated in those awakenings. The most important point to make from this is that awakening with panic is not necessarily an unexplainable event but may be very directly related to bodily sensations that are frightening. Jill reported that quite regularly she would wake up in the middle of the night feeling very frightened. It seemed to her that the first thing she would notice upon

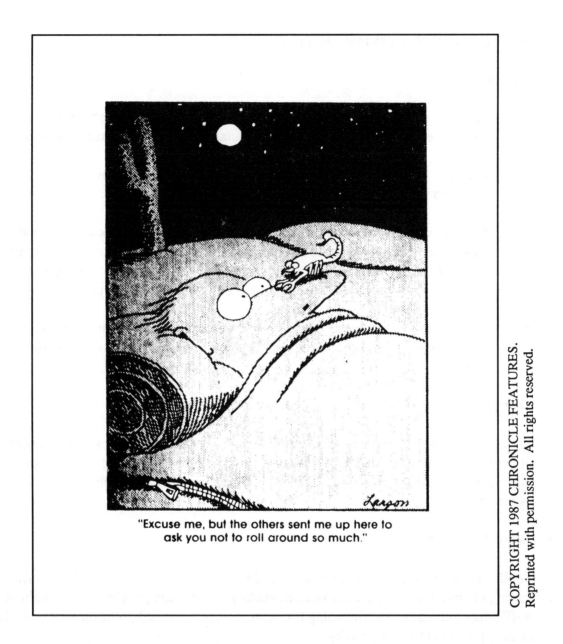

"Excuse me, but the others sent me up here to ask you not to roll around so much."

awakening was a racing heart and that scared her. General anxiety is often related to restless sleep and awakenings. However, whereas someone who is generally anxious but not afraid of bodily senations might respond to the wakenings with frustration, another person who is cued into physical sensations is more likely to respond to the wakening with fear. Similarly, becoming relaxed and feeling comfortable at home is sometimes associated with dwelling on oneself, or body scanning, and feeling sensations that are normal that you would not otherwise notice because your attention is focused elsewhere. Some people also experience a feeling of loss of control when they relax deeply. Therefore, in this case of relaxation induced anxiety or panic, the panic cues would result from focusing of attention on sensations. It is likely that you have times when you experience predicted or expected episodes of anxiety and/or panic. That is, you might expect to experience anxiety in response to specific external situations where you have felt anxious before, such as crowded shopping malls or being alone at home or driving a car, etc. The other times, when you become anxious or panic and were not expecting to do so, are likely to be related to the following list of cues which are less obvious than external situations:

(1) Physical State

    a)   Feeling natural sensations that have been associated with anxiety or panic in the past and, therefore, currently can trigger an anxious mode of thinking and feeling when noticed. For example, feeling breathlessness or racing of the heart from physical exercise; feeling nauseous from overeating or "bad food", alcohol or ill health; feeling hot from the heat of the sun; shaking from the cold, and so on.

    b)   Feeling natural sensations that have not necessarily been associated with anxiety or panic in the past but which are misinterpreted as signs of anxiety or panic. For example, states of fatigue, hunger, thirst, frustration, and anger have sometimes been misinterpreted as signs of anxiety and, therefore, begin the spiral into panic.

    c)   Feeling sensations that are due to high levels of physiological arousal associated with high levels of general anxiety such as muscle tension, racing heart, sweating and trembling.

(2) Thoughts

Thoughts are not only important after the anxious cycle has begun but can also trigger anxious or panicky feelings. For example, worrying about one's ability to cope with anxiety, thinking about the possibility of panicking again, and worrying about upcoming events can all serve as precipitants.

(3) General Stressors

Subtle pressures, which are both positive and negative in nature, can build to contribute to a feeling of anxiety or panic. For example, dealing with hostile people, being caught in heavy traffic, meeting a deadline, finalizing financial arrangements and going on a date can all serve as precipitants to feeling panicky.

Over the next week, spend time evaluating the likely precipitants every time you feel anxious or panicky. Go through the list given above to determine whether any of those elements were involved in the development of the anxiety or fear reaction.

Exercise

Continue to monitor your anxiety and panic using the DAILY MOOD and PANIC ATTACK records. Continue to use relaxation and/or breathing retraining when feeling anxious and tense. Continue to challenge overestimations and catastrophic self-statements at the end of each day by reviewing your episodes of anxiety and panic during the course of the day. For every episode, also determine the trigger events, using the checklist provided above. Continue in this way for a full week before proceeding to the next chapter.

Self-Assessment

Answer each of the following by circling true (T) or false (F). Answers are on page A-4 - A-5.

1. The experience of an unexpected panic is an indication
    that the precipitant was not obvious.   T   F

2. Unexpected panic attacks are more threatening than those
    which are expected.   T   F

3. If you do not successfully apply methods of relaxation
    or breathing, then you are in dire trouble.   T   F

4. Situations are not the only precipitants to panic;
    other precipitants which are more subtle include physical
    sensations, thoughts and general stressors.   T   F

CHAPTER 10

Producing the Panic Sensations

Review

Review your last week's DAILY MOOD and PANIC ATTACK records and add the average anxiety and number of panic attacks to your PROGRESS RECORD. Spend a few minutes thinking about any patterns that developed. Do you understand each episode of anxiety and/or panic in terms of response components and sequencing? Do you understand your emotional reactions in an objective manner? Also, record your evidence-based judgments of probability and ability to cope on your SELF-STATEMENT RATING form. Have your estimates changed?

Response Component Strategies

Review your use of either breathing retraining and/or relaxation and self-statement modification over the preceding week. Ensure that you are applying the strategies when tension or anxiety are first noticed. Also, check your predictions from the preceding week on the PREDICTION TESTING form. Determine the degree to which your predictions were accurate. In most cases, you will find that the things that you were worried about did not occur. Therefore, your prediction was inaccurate. That is, you were able to drive despite feeling anxious or dizzy and you were able to walk through the mall despite feeling lightheaded. Now make a new set of predictions for events that will occur during the subsequent week and record your predictions on the PREDICTION TESTING form. Remember to rate according to how you usually feel in those particular situations. Don't subject your concerns to logical analysis for these particular ratings. Finally, review your attempts to conduct an analysis of causes for every time you felt anxious or panicky. Did you at least analyze causes at the end of the day for all the episodes of anxiety or panic that occurred during the day? Were you able to identify possible cues that explained the panic spiral even though it initially seemed to be an unexpected response? Were there subtle physical sensations of which you became aware? Were there certain thoughts that came into your mind that started off the spiral? Were there a lot of stressors going on that generally made you feel more anxious and, in turn, more aware of the possibility of panic and, therefore, more sensitive to minor physical fluctuations.

Producing the Panic Sensation

The element that is central to panic is a fearful reaction to somatic sensations (e.g., racing heart, dizziness, etc.). We do the following exercise near the end because it is very difficult for some people to do and we want to be sure that you have mastered the previous exercises and have learned how to control your physical sensations and thoughts. It is now time to test your reactivity to different panic sensations.

Individuals differ in the particular sensations that frighten them most. We use a series of exercises that bring on sensations similar to the sensations experienced during anxiety and panic. The goal of the series of exercises is to allow you to determine the exercises which are most relevant to you and which can be practiced regularly for best results. The goal of these practices will be to decrease or eliminate your fear of the somatic sensations. Fear reduction can only be accomplished by repeatedly confronting the things that frighten you, in this case, the bodily sensations. Just as when you are frightened of an animal or crossing a bridge, it is important to face your fear, at least a little bit at a time.

In addition, performance of these exercises will provide you a chance to practice more purposely the strategies that you have acquired up to this point: breathing retraining or relaxation training, and self-statement modification. Although you should continue to use those strategies upon feeling anxious in your day to day life, their application during these repeated practices will enhance their effectiveness and their preparedness. That is, the more you rehearse a particular strategy, the more powerful and natural it becomes.

First, we will begin by practicing specific exercises. Then, we will extend these exercises to activities in your day to day life. Finally, we will extend the activities to particular situations that have become anxiety provoking for you. Let's begin with the specific exercises.

The goal is for you to identify any sensations that you feel as a result of each exercise. Once you have identified the sensations, it will be very important to rate 3 different aspects of the sensations: First, the intensity of the sensations (which is rated on a 0-8 point scale where 0 = not at all and 8 = extreme); second, the level of anxiety or fear you experience in response to those sensations (on a 0-8 point scale where 0 = none at all and 8 = extreme); and third, how similar those sensations are to the sensations that you would experience in a natural episode of anxiety or panic (on a 0-8 point scale where 0 = not at all similar and 8 = exactly the same). If you are working with your doctor or mental health professional, he or she can demonstrate each exercise for you. Otherwise, you can attempt each exercise in your living room but have someone with you the first time you do the exercises. The set of exercises are listed below:

1. Shaking your head from side to side for 30 seconds.

2. Placing your head between your legs for 30 seconds and then lifting to an upright position quickly.

3. Take one step up, using stairs or a box or a footstool, and immediately step down. Do this repeatedly at a fast enough rate to notice your heart pumping quickly for one minute.

4. Holding your breath for 30 seconds.

5. Complete body muscle tension for one minute. Tense every part of your body, without causing pain. Tense your arms, legs, stomach, back, shoulders, face - everything. Alternatively, try holding a push-up position for one minute, or as long as you can.

6. Spinning in a chair for one minute. If you have a chair that spins such as a desk chair, this is ideal. It's even better if someone is there to spin you around. Otherwise, stand up and turn around quickly to make yourself dizzy. Be near a soft chair or couch that you can sit in immediately after one minute is up.

7. Hyperventilating for one minute. Breathe deep and fast - use a lot of force. Sit down as you do this.

8. Breathe through a thin straw for one minute. Don't allow any air through your nose; hold your nostrils together.

Other individually tailored exercises can be designed to suit your own pattern of responding. For example, if you are most distressed by visual distortions, practice staring at the same spot for two minutes or practice looking at a light for 30 seconds and then looking at a blank wall to experience the after-image. If you are concerned mainly upon throat sensations, practice putting pressure against the sides of your throat or pressing down on the back of your tongue. Another exercise is to sit in a hot, stuffy room or car for five minutes. You should know by now which are the sensations that scare you most, so be creative and invent some ways to produce those sensations. It is essential that you experience the sensations most important for you. When Jill performed each of the standard exercises, she experienced the following:

1. Head shaking

"Wow - that makes me feel dizzy and disoriented. My eyes are out of focus - but now they are coming back into focus."
For Jill, this exercise did not produce much fear (2), nor were the sensations rated as being very similar to her natural anxiety or panic sensations (2). Nevertheless, she rated the sensations at the end of the procedure as quite intense (6).

2. Head lift

"I feel a little dizzy and lightheaded. This was not much at all."
She did not report any fear (1), nor much similarity (2), and rated the sensation intensity as being quite mild (3).

3. Step ups - Jill stopped this one after 45 seconds.

"I feel like I have to stop - my heart is beating fast, and I feel sweaty and out of breath. Usually, I try to avoid doing any exercise."
Jill rated this procedure as producing sensations that were very intense (7), very similar to what she felt during her panic attacks (6), and, initially, she felt quite frightened (5).

4. Breath holding

"Nothing - just a little chest pressure."
Jill's ratings were all mild.

5. <u>Complete tension</u>
"I feel a little shaky and trembly, and I also feel weak."
While the sensations were quite intense for Jill (5), she did not fear them (1) and rated the similarity as being low (1).

6. <u>Spinning</u> - Jill stopped this after 30 seconds.
"Boy, I feel really dizzy. The room is spinning - I am spinning. And my heart is racing and I feel sweaty. It's calming down now."
These sensations were very intense (7), similar to those she felt when she panicked (5) and frightening (4).

7. <u>Hyperventilation</u> - Jill stopped after 45 seconds.
"I feel really hot and sweaty, tingly in my face, lightheaded and like I need to take a deep breath."
Again, this procedure produced sensations that Jill rated as being very intense (7), similar to her natural panics (5) and frightening (6).

8. <u>Restricted breathing</u> - Jill stopped after 35 seconds.
"I feel like I can't keep going, I have to take a deep breath."
Jill rated the symptoms as being intense (6), quite similar to her panic symptoms (4) and frightening (6).

Now, attempt each exercise and then look at your list of responses. Star (*) the exercises which produced symptoms that you rated as being at least 3 on the 0-8 point scale of similarity. Rank the starred exercises in order of the level of anxiety that they produce. The repeated practices will begin with the exercise that has the least anxiety or fear associated with it (but which has a similarity of at least 3). So, Jill's exercises were ranked as follows: first, spinning; second, step ups; third, hyper-ventilating; and forth, straw breathing. It would be helpful if you had a timing device next to you as you do the exercises. For the repeated practice, the following procedure is to be used. Remember, that it is important to practice each one repeatedly because that is how fear reduces. When you first notice the sensations produced by the exercise, it is <u>very</u> <u>important</u> to continue with the procedure for an additional 30 seconds (10 seconds in the case of holding your breath and shaking your head). At the end of that time, stop the exercise procedure and then rate the intensity of your anxiety or fear on the 0-8 point scale, using the EXPOSURE RECORD shown on Table 10:1. Make lots of copies of this form as you will be using it a great deal over the next three lessons.

Then, after you make your ratings, apply either breathing retraining or relaxation techniques (whatever you have been using) and identify any anxiety provoking self-statements and modify them using the strategies we have used before. This is where you get to practice your strategies. Be particularly aware of anxiety-provoking statements such as "I have to stop - I can't tolerate these feelings." That is a prediction you are making which is based on fear only - you can, in fact, tolerate and continue the procedures.

Do not attempt to apply any strategies (physical or self-statement strategies) <u>before</u> the exercise procedure. It is important that you experience fully the sensations, and then allow the anxiety/fear

Table 10:1

Exercise Exposure Record

Day	Exercise	Trial	Anxiety/Fear 0-8
_____	_____	_____	_____
_____	_____	_____	_____
_____	_____	_____	_____
_____	_____	_____	_____
_____	_____	_____	_____
_____	_____	_____	_____
_____	_____	_____	_____
_____	_____	_____	_____
_____	_____	_____	_____

"It's OK! It's OK! The tunnel was closing in on me there for a while, but I'm all right now."

to reduce through repeated controlled exposures. Although you have been instructed to implement the panic management strategies (self-statement analysis, breathing retraining or relaxation) upon first noticing physical symptoms or anxiety in your daily life, now it is time to experience the symptoms fully and, subsequently, apply the management skills.

It is important that you attempt to elicit the sensations as <u>strongly</u> as you can. Do not avoid the sensations by performing the exercises very mildly. Don't be too cautious. The importance of experiencing the sensations intensely cannot be emphasized enough. For example, during the step ups, the pace must be fast enough to experience definite cardiovascular symptoms. While spinning, the turning must be continuous so that dizziness is produced. When hyperventilating, ensure that the air is forced out with a lot of pressure and the breathing rate is fast (you are unlikely to pass out from the hyperventilation unless you extend longer than ten minutes). You will defeat the purpose of the procedure if you don't try really hard.

If none of the exercises produce fear, despite the similarity of the sensations to sensations you would experience naturally, determine whether one or both of the following issues prevails:

(1)   You are not fearful or anxious because you feel safe in the particular setting in which you perform the exercise. Some of our clients report that if they had to do these exercises when alone, they would be more frightened, but when accompanied they feel safe because if anything happens there would be someone there to help them. Note that this fear is based on the inaccurate assumption that they are in danger if alone, when in fact these exercises are no more dangerous when alone than when accompanied.

(2)   The sensations are not as frightening because you feel you have control over their onset. Some of our clients state that because they know exactly where the sensations come from, they are not frightened. Note that this fear is based on the assumption that natural panics do not have specific triggers - but you know better, right!

If either of these issues are operating, it would be helpful to combine the exercise with some use of your imagination. As you experience the sensations, try to imagine yourself as vividly as you can within a frightening situation. For example, imagine yourself at home alone with no one nearby who could help while you hyperventilate. If that still does not result in feeling anxious or fearful, then it will simply be important for you to practice the exercises when you are actually alone. Only by doing this will you really learn to be less frightened of the sensations.

Repeat the same exercise the number of times that it is necessary in order for the anxiety/fear level to reduce to 2 or less on the 0-8 point scale. Remember that the anxiety/fear is rated in terms of the maximum level you felt either during the exercise or immediately after you stopped the exercise. Wait until your physical symptoms have abated and you no longer feel anxious or afraid before you repeat the exercise. If your anxiety/fear does not reduce to two after five trials, then stop practicing and start again the next day, otherwise you will just exhaust yourself. An example of Jill's EXPOSURE RECORD is provided below indicating at what point a specific exercise has been practiced enough. When the anxiety/fear level reaches two or less, move on to the next exercise which is to be chosen on the basis of the level of maximum anxiety/fear that was recorded initially. That is, choose the exercise associated with the second lowest level of anxiety/fear when you first tried each exercise. Again, using exactly the same techniques as specified before, continue to repeat the exercise until the anxiety/fear rating is two or less. As it is very important to consolidate the anxiety reduction effects, you will be asked to practice the first two exercises daily over the next week.

Jill practiced the following exercises:

(1) Spinning
(2) Step ups
(3) Hyperventilating
(4) Straw breathing

In the clinic, she found, like almost all of our clients, that her anxiety levels quickly reduced.

Table 10:2
JILL'S EXERCISE
EXPOSURE RECORD

Day	Exercise	Trial	Anxiety/Fear 0-8
Day 1	Spinning	1	6
	"	2	5
	"	3	3
	"	4	2
	Step ups	1	5
	"	2	4
	"	3	2
Day 2	Hyperventilation	1	6
	"	2	6
	"	3	5
	"	4	5
	"	5	4
Day 3	Hyperventilation	1	5
	"	2	4
	"	3	4
	"	4	3
	"	5	2
	Straw breathing	1	5
		2	4
		3	3
		4	2

The third time she spun, although she stated that the sensations were still intense, she was only mildly fearful. She even spun for a longer time. The fourth time, her anxiety rating was only a two. When she first practiced alone, the fear was a little higher (a four the first time). However, as when in the clinic, the fear reduced as she continued to practice alone. As with many people, Jill's anxiety/fear levels were a little higher, after several days without practice. That is nothing to be worried about, as it just signifies the need for more practice. With regular practice you will find that in your day to day life, when you do notice different sensations occurring because you feel uptight or whatever, you will be less frightened of them. This has two consequences - the sensations will not intensify and you will feel more control.

Jill needed to practice hyperventilation over two days, because initially she felt that she could not tolerate the symptoms. It was important for her to learn that although the symptoms are not comfortable, they are not unbearable and can be tolerated. Initially, Jill would anxiously wait for the dizziness to abate and, therefore, she added tension and prolonged the intensity of the symptoms. However, after a couple of days of practicing (five times each day), she reached the point of realizing that the symptoms were tolerable and, therefore, they in fact decreased much more quickly.

Exercise

Do each of the following over the next seven days.

(1)   Continue use of breathing retraining and/or relaxation upon awareness of tension, anxiety or panic.

(2)   Continue to identify and modify anxiety provoking self-statements. Perform this analysis at the end of each day but also try to apply this process to times when you are anxious or panicky.

(3)   Continue an analysis of causes of anxiety and panic episodes.

(4)   Daily practice of exercises that were conducted in this session. Don't put this off - practice every day if you want to get the most benefit. Repeat a single exercise the number of times it is necessary in order to experience a level of maximum anxiety/fear no greater than two. Record your levels of anxiety on the EXERCISE EXPOSURE RECORD. Remember to apply the somatic and self-statement strategies after the exercise procedure. Go on to the next exercise when your anxiety for the first exercise reduces to two. However, do no more than two different exercises - just repeat each of the two exercises daily. If neither of them produce a level of anxiety greater than two after a certain number of days, just continue to do them both two times each day until a full week has passed. And, remember, do each exercise with the intention of producing strong sensations. Don't avoid the feelings. Read the instructions in this chapter very carefully to ensure correct procedures are used.

Self-Assessment

Answer the following by circling true (T) or false (F). Answers are on page A-5.

(1)   It is important to experience the sensations to the
      fullest and to allow the anxiety to be experienced
      fully when you practice the various exercises.   T   F

(2)   All individuals respond in exactly the same way to
      these exercises.   T   F

(3)   Repeat the exercises the number of times it is
      necessary for the level of anxiety to reduce to a 2 on
      the 0-8 point scale.   T   F

(4)   Try to prevent the anxiety from developing before you
      do the exercises by applying breathing retraining and
      self-statement modification.   T   F

CHAPTER 11

Producing Panic Sensations in your Daily Life

Review

Review your DAILY MOOD and PANIC ATTACK records. Add the average anxiety and number of panic attacks to your PROGRESS RECORD. Review your application of either breathing retraining or relaxation techniques and cognitive modification. Did you use an analysis of causes? What about your predictions? Check your PREDICTION TESTING form. How accurate were you last week? What can you learn from this information? Have your estimates altered? Add your evidence-based judgments of probability and ability to cope to your SELF-STATEMENT RATING form. Have you become more confident in your ability to cope and/or less worried about certain things happening? Did you practice daily the exercises introduced in the last chapter? Were you able to notice changes in the level of anxiety/fear with repeated practice? If the practices did not produce any anxiety or fear, did you perform the exercise while imagining yourself in a threatening situation (where "threatening" is based on your perception rather than objective threat)? Did you apply the exercises as described or were you avoidant? It is important that you produce the sensations to the fullest degree. Did you employ any forms of distraction while you were bringing on the sensations, such as thinking about other events? If so, stop the distraction because that prevents the benefit of the exposure. It is essential that you experience everything to the fullest in order to benefit from this procedure.

Continued Exercise Exposure

Now continue on your hierarchy of exercises by moving to the next fear-producing exercise. Use the same procedures as specified previously. That is, practice the exercise until you notice the sensations. Remember to continue the exercise for at least 30 seconds longer (or 10 seconds in the case of shaking your head and holding your breath) after the sensations are first noticed. Then record the intensity of the anxiety/fear. Then apply your strategies to reduce the fear and anxiety. Once you feel physically and emotionally calm repeat the exercise. Repeat the exercise the number of times that it is necessary in order for the maximum anxiety/fear rating to reach two or less. Then continue with the next exercise. Continue in this way until you have completed all of the exercises listed on your hierarchy. Remember to include different exercises that are relevant to your areas of sensitivity. Don't leave out the exercises of which you are most frightened because they induce feelings very similar to your panic attacks. Over the following week, practice the exercises daily. Repeat each one the number of times that it is necessary for the anxiety to reduce to two, using the EXPOSURE RECORD form to monitor your progress. So, for example, it may take you two days to reach an anxiety/fear level of two with a particular exercise and then on the third day you would start practicing a new exercise repeatedly until the anxiety level reaches two. Remember, don't do any more than five trials on any one day. Remember also to separate unpleasantness from anxiety or fear. While feeling dizzy may never be a pleasant sensation (although some would disagree!), it can be experienced and tolerated without fear. If none of the exercises produce a level of fear greater than two by the middle of the week, just repeat each one twice each day.

Activities Exposure

The extension of this procedure is to apply the same kind of approach to natural activities that induce sensations similar to the sensations that you experience during panic. It is possible that you have developed avoidance of certain activities because they produce sensations which are frightening to you, although you may not be aware of the avoidance. Examples of such activities include the following: drinking coffee (because of the stimulant effect), eating chocolate (because of the stimulant or expected stimulant effect), aerobic activity (because of the cardiovascular effect), lifting heavy objects - or an anaerobic activity (because of the heightened blood pressure and dizziness effects), moving your body position quickly, running up flights of stairs, hot and stuffy rooms, having a shower with the door closed, going into saunas, watching horror movies, having sexual relations, walking outside in very cold air, walking outside in intense heat, hiking, sports, eating heavy meals and so on. Examine each of these and other similar activities and assess whether you have either been avoiding the activities or doing them but with hesitation and fear because of the sensations they produce. This is a good example of the way in which sensations cue panic attacks even though they are not immediately perceived as being the reason for panicking at any given time (analysis of causes). Next lesson we will begin practicing those kinds of activities. Before the next lesson, identify and list all activities in your daily life that you have avoided or feel afraid of doing because of the induction of sensations. A sample list is provided.

What To Do If Anxiety and Panic Recur

It is natural for anxiety and panic to recur from time to time during treatment. By its nature, this problem is one that waxes and wanes so there will be times during treatment when panic attacks return, even if they have disappeared for a while. The recurrence of episodes of intense anxiety and panic is simply an indication that the anxious thoughts, tendency to overbreathe, physical tension, and sensitivity to sensations are still present. As mentioned previously, the strategies for reducing your physical sensations and monitoring and modifying your cognitions are designed to break the response cycle of fear and panic. They are not "bandaid" techniques that cover underlying panic, but they are strategies which disintegrate the experience of panic. Also, repeated exposures to the sensations will reduce your sensitivity so that when different sensations arise, fear is much less likely to occur and, indeed, your awareness of those sensations, in general, will reduce. This, in turn, will reduce your level of general anxiety, which means a lowered possibility of experiencing sensations in the first place. However, it is still likely that you may experience times of intense anxiety and panic, especially in novel or demanding situations where it's easier to revert to old habits. But it is very important to put that into proper perspective. It is not an indication of failure or relapse but simply a signal that there is still, within your emotional structure, an element that requires further work. This is the normal pattern. Progress through treatment is never one of steady improvement, but the times of panic allow more learning to take place. So, believe it or not, having panics is beneficial for your treatment.

You might feel that it is harder to apply fear management strategies at times when you are extremely anxious. That is true. However, there are key elements for you to remember which would help you to maintain a more objective focus rather than being caught up in the emotional cycle of fear. That is, management at this level still requires interruption of the cycle of the emotional response.

<u>Table 11:1</u>

Daily Activities That Produce Panic Sensations

Running up flights of stairs

Walking outside in intense heat

Hot, stuffy rooms

Hot, stuffy cars

Hot, stuffy stores, or shopping malls

Walking outside in very cold weather

Aerobics

Lifting heavy objects

Dancing

Sexual relations

Watching horror movies

Eating heavy meals

Watching exciting movies or sports events

Getting involved in "heated" debates

Having showers with the doors and windows closed

Having a sauna

Hiking

Sports

Drinking coffee, caffeinated beverages

Eating chocolate

Standing quickly from a sitting position

Getting angry

The following are the kinds of problems that are sometimes reported at points of high anxiety and panic:

1.   The panic is so sudden that I do not have time to think.

2.   I feel so distraught that I cannot think clearly or logically.

3.   At those times when I am feeling very panicky, it is hard to believe the alternative self-statements and my belief in the negative statements increases (i.e., I really am going to die).

4.   I just cannot control my physical tension or breathing patterns.

Identify which of those four processes, or any others, occur at times of intense fear and panic and which seem to hinder appropriate control. For each of those issues, the following key points should be remembered:

1.   Ask yourself a series of key questions to help you become more objective, such as "What are my thoughts?", "What is the worst that can happen?" "What is the likelihood of that happening?", "What was the precipitant to this episode?," "How have my reactions spiralled into the feeling of panic?", etc.

2.   Remember that despite the _feeling_ that what you are most afraid of (e.g., losing control) will actually occur and/or actually be catastrophic, this feeling is transient, is motivated by a set of inaccurate beliefs, and that the same concerns have predominated at previous panic times yet have never happened.

3.   Continue to attempt to reduce the physical sensations by breathing retraining or relaxation techniques, but remember, even if you feel that you cannot control your breathing patterns or your physical tension, it really does not matter because the symptoms are harmless anyway.

Write the important points on a small card that can be carried with you and used as an external prompt at times when you become very panicky. Having that external prompt will help you to become an objective observer of the sequence of events, which in turn allows you to be more in control of your reactions rather than feeling caught up in the emotional response cycle.

Exercise

Over the next seven days,

1. Continue the use of breathing retraining or relaxation training, self-statement modification and analysis of causes.

2. Daily practice of the specific exercises with repetition of each exercise until the anxiety or fear is reduced to a level of two. During these exercises, experience the sensations to the fullest before applying your management strategies.

3. Identification of activities that you avoid or that you engage in with fear because they elicit sensations that remind you of the feeling of panic.

4. Use of several key external prompting questions and statements at times when you feel extremely panicky. Write these on a card to be carried with you and used at times of heightened anxiety or panic.

Self-Assessment

Answer each of the following by circling true (T) or false (F). Answers are on page A-5.

1. Experiencing panic at this point means that I am seriously ill or that I've lost everything that I have gained.   T   F

2. Remember to ask myself key questions at times when the fear level is intense.   T   F

3. I should try to fight off the feeling of fear at all cost.   T   F

4. The more I practice the exercises, the more benefit I will get from the treatment.   T   F

CHAPTER 12

Producing Panic Sensations in your Daily Life - Continued

Review

Review your DAILY MOOD and PANIC ATTACK RECORDS and add the average anxiety and number of panic attacks to your PROGRESS RECORD. Review your use of the various strategies including somatic reduction, self-statement modification and analysis of causes. What about your estimates of the probability that certain terrible things will happen or that you wouldn't be able to cope? Add your estimates for this week to your SELF-STATEMENT RATING form. Look at the changes that have occurred in your estimates. Did you practice the sensation producing exercises daily? Did your level of fear reduce in response to each exercise? Were you able to apply the questions and key statements (written on a card) at times when you felt extreme anxiety or panic? A main point to remember is that fear in and of itself is harmless and even if you did nothing, it would reduce on its own. In other words, the fear is transient and at times of intense anxiety or panic, the techniques of somatic and cognitive change will simply speed up the fear reduction process.

Confrontation With Fear in your Daily Life

Were you able to produce a list of activities that you have been avoiding or in which you feel frightened because of the physical sensations these activities produce? Now, rank all of those activities in terms of how much anxiety or fear is associated with each one, using the 0 to 8 point scale. This is now your hierarchy and, as with the exercise procedures over the last two weeks, the goal is to repeat each activity the number of times that is necessary for you to experience very mild levels of anxiety. This requires a lot of effort and work because often these activities take more time to complete than the previous exercises.

However, it is important for you to remember that the more effort you put into doing these exercises and practices the more you will benefit. That is a known fact. You may be able to engage the help of a friend or family member at this point to provide extra motivation for doing these practices. As with the previous exercises, it is important that you record the level of maximum anxiety/fear you experience for each activity. Then, apply the strategies as discussed during this program (i.e., relaxation or breathing, and self-statements). When you feel physically and emotionally calm, repeat the activity again. The repetition can be done either immediately after the first practice or a longer time after. That depends somewhat on the particular activity. For example, while sitting in a hot, stuffy room can be repeated fairly quickly, eating certain foods may require longer intervals for practical reasons. Give the time intervals between practices some thought. It might take two weeks or longer for you to go through your hierarchy of activities. It is very important that you practice regularly. Do not put it off!

There is a difference between the exercises done previously and the natural activities that you will be completing over the next few weeks. It is very clear that the symptoms are produced by the exercises (such as spinning and hyperventilating) and that the symptoms stop as soon as the exercises are stopped. It is likely that with naturalistic activities the onset and the offset of the symptoms will

**Professor Gallagher and his controversial
technique of simultaneously confronting the
fear of heights, snakes, and the dark**

be less clear. However, that is not a cause for further fear and anxiety. It is simply a function of the fact that activities are not as predictable as the exercises in terms of eliciting the symptoms, and that they may be associated with more anticipatory anxiety because of your expectations. For example, you may have a lot of anticipation about drinking a cup of coffee because you expect to experience the symptoms. In addition, the symptoms may not occur straight away because it takes some time for the caffeine to circulate and for its effect to develop. Furthermore, you cannot predict exactly when those symptoms will diminish. If you focus on the symptoms, waiting for them to go away and worrying about them, then indeed the symptoms will last longer because you are feeding the anxiety/ fear response. In other words, just be aware that the symptoms may occur differently than during the specific exercises conducted before, but it is still important for you to experience them to the fullest degree and learn to be less frightened by them when they do occur.

Remember also that the goal of this treatment is to reduce your sensitivity to physical symptoms, whether they be directly predictable and controllable or not. The fact that the symptoms are prolonged does not mean that they are any more dangerous. If you notice your heart racing after drinking a cup of coffee and then focus on your heart and start to feel that you are in danger, of course your heart will continue to race for a longer period of time. This will happen because you are giving yourself fearful information, and one of the effects of being afraid is to experience a racing heart. So, over the next few weeks, plan for daily activities (or, as close to daily as you can), starting with the ones that produce the least anxiety and continuing with each one until it no longer produces more than a rating of two on your anxiety/fear scale. Then, repeat the whole procedure with the next activity. Use the same EXPOSURE RECORD form that you used before to monitor your practices and fear levels. Remember to expect to experience different sensations when you attempt these activities; don't "hope that you won't feel dizzy or shaky". Expect the symptoms and learn to be less fearful of them.

Jill's activities for her first two weeks were to practice attending a fitness class (ten minutes each time), first with a friend and then alone, and to have a shower with the curtain drawn and door closed. Her initial ratings of fear level for each activity were three, four and five, respectively. Her ratings are shown below on her EXPOSURE RECORD form. The first time she joined the fitness class, she experienced a considerable amount of anticipation before the class but practiced slow, diaphramatic breathing and reinforced the specific information that although she may feel out of

Table 12:1

**Jill's
Activity
Exposure Record**

Activity	Trial	Anxiety/Fear 0-8
10 minutes in fitness class		
- with friend	1	5
	2	4
	3	2
	4	2
- alone	1	5
	2	5
	3	4
	4	2
Showering with curtain drawn and door closed	1	4
	2	3
	3	3
	4	2

breath, hot, sweaty and have a racing heart, she was not in danger by doing the exercises at a sensible pace. While actually in the fitness class, Jill experienced, at one point, the feeling that she "had to stop and leave the class", but when she realized that by going at her own pace she was actually able to tolerate the feelings and was not in danger, she stayed for the full ten minutes. It is very important to control the feeling of wanting to run away or get to safety. After the first practice, Jill found it became easier and she even stayed for longer periods in the class, and started to attend class alone. Similarly, her fears in the shower reduced with practice.

Dealing with Frightening Memories

An additional method of exposing yourself systematically and repeatedly to panic-related issues and, therefore, learning to be less afraid, is to remember the worst panic that you've ever experienced. Sometimes, the memory of a particular event can be very biased. The bias can serve to maintain the fear. For example, let's say that ten years ago you were bitten by a dog and that experience was extremely traumatic. Every now and then the memory comes back to you and you feel frightened as you think of it. As a consequence, it is much more likely that the next time you see a dog, you will be frightened. In contrast, if ten years ago you had been bitten by a dog but no longer had a memory of it as being a terrible or catastrophic experience but rather just an unpleasant event, and as a consequence the event is rarely remembered, then it is likely that the next time you see a dog, you will not be anywhere near as frightened as in the first case. An important part of this process is that whenever a past event is given a lot of significance (such as when thought of as horrible, catastrophic, etc.), it is more easily recalled in your mind. The more frequently you recall and feel distressed by the memory, the stronger it becomes. Therefore, if you think of the worst panic that you have ever had, remembering it as being terrifying, excruciating and something you never ever want to go through again and, in fact, it makes you feel frightened as you think about it, and for that reason you have tended to avoid thinking about it, then it will be important for you to "process" that memory and make it a much less significant element in your consciousness. Many of the clients who have attended our clinic have become less generally anxious and less on edge, waiting for their next panic, when they have learned to understand their past panics rather than just be horrified by them. This is accomplished by forcing yourself to deliberately and fully think about the experience a number of times in a very objective way. It entails doing the kind of sequential analysis that you have already practiced.

First, try to recall the worst panic and, as clearly as you can, remember the context including the people, the place, the sounds around you, the colors, the objects that you can see, and anything else that is characteristic of the place. Try to imagine it as clearly as you can by placing yourself in the picture, not as an observer but as someone participating in the scene. Try to remember how you felt. Remember the sequence of events. What was the first thing that happened? What was your reaction to that? What was the reaction of the other people? How did you feel? What was the next step? You might, indeed, become quite anxious or fearful as you think about that event, but don't stop, keep thinking about it. Ask yourself if there are any of the following kinds of statements going through your mind as you think about that panic: "I hate to even think about it", "I hope I never experience anything like that again", "I couldn't go through that again", "I'm sure I nearly died," "I was so lucky to survive", etc. If those statements or similar kinds of statements characterize the way you feel, then it is very important that you go through a process of continued exposure to the memory.

Think about the event again, particularly the way you felt. Ask yourself to identify the possible antecedents that began the whole cycle including possible sensations, thoughts, or general stressors. Once the precipitant had occurred and you began to react, what were the physical reactions that you experienced? What was the first physical sensation that you noticed? How did you react to that sensation? What thoughts came into your mind? Did you make any over-estimations (e.g. did you think that you were going to die) or did you become catastrophic (e.g. did you feel that everyone would notice and think you were crazy)? What was the next thing that happened? Did you become more frightened? Try to understand the sequence of events and how the physical sensations and thoughts fed into each other? What did you do? Did you go to an emergency room, or try to escape, or call for help or lie down? How did each of those activities add into the fear cycle? Did they serve to confirm to you that you were in danger, for example? Now again, try to evaluate how you think about that event overall. Indeed, it may have been a surprising event, and it may have been very unpleasant and frightening at the time, but that doesn't mean that if you were in the same circumstances, feeling the same sensations, that you would respond in the same way. Go through the memory once more and continue to do so, asking yourself the questions that were outlined above, until you can think about that event without the memory making you feel very anxious.

Exercise

1. Plan the activities that you are going to practice over the next couple of weeks. Make sure that you practice everyday (or almost everyday) and that you repeat a given activity the number of times that it is necessary in order for the fear to reduce to a level of two. Remember to design the sequence of practices according to each particular activity (i.e., sitting in a hot, stuffy room can be practiced repeatedly without long intervening rest periods, whereas showering or eating certain foods may require longer intervals between practices). Keep a record of your anxiety/fear levels, using the EXPOSURE RECORD FORM.

2. If you find that your memories of past panics make you feel very frightened, practice thinking about past panic attacks and asking yourself key questions that will enable you to understand objectively the sequence of what happened and how the panic developed. Continue to review past panic attacks until you no longer feel distressed by the memory of those events.

Self-Assessment

Answer each of the following by circling true (T) or false (F). Answers are on page A-6.

1. If thinking about my worst panic makes me feel anxious,
   I should avoid thinking about it.   T   F

2. I should practice each activity daily in order to get
   the most benefit and the number of repetitions is based
   on the level of anxiety I feel.   T   F

3. If the sensations continue for a long time, that does
   not mean that they are any more threatening. It is
   likely that I am focusing on the sensations and becoming
   worried by them in a way that is unjustified.   T   F

4. I should proceed with each activity in my hierarchy
   starting from the activity associated with the lowest
   level of anxiety.   T   F

CHAPTER 13

Overcoming Your Phobic Avoidance: Producing Panic Sensations in Agoraphobic Situations

Review

Review your DAILY MOOD and PANIC ATTACK RECORDS over the past two weeks. Add the average anxiety and number of panic attacks per week to your PROGRESS RECORD. Spend a few minutes examining whether any different patterns have emerged in either the frequency, intensity or sequencing of your episodes of panic. Ask yourself whether you are still afraid of experiencing a "panic". If so, return to some of the previous chapters and review the material that has been presented. A continuing fear of panic suggests that there still needs to be some work done on your understanding of what is panic. Go through the three response system analysis once again. Describe your most recent panic in terms of the physical sensations, the subjective feelings and thoughts and your behavior. What are the major triggers that begin your feeling of fear? What is the first thing that happens? What is your reaction to that and how does the sequence spiral into a feeling of intense fear, which is then called panic? Also, rate your evidence-based estimates of probability and ability to cope with your most distressing anticipated events when panicking and when feeling generally anxious, using your SELF-STATEMENT RATING form. Have your estimates changed? Do you believe the events are less likely to occur and/or that you are more able to cope if they did occur?

Review your application of strategies designed to correct your misinterpretations and to correct your levels of physical tension or irregular breathing. Have you been able to implement those strategies at times when you notice yourself either physically uptight or thinking fearful thoughts? Remember not to use those strategies as a method of escape or of fighting off the anxiety. They are not designed to "prevent at all costs" the feeling of fear. Also, remember not to use those methods as a way of distracting yourself from your feelings. They are designed to alter or modify the subjective and the physical components of your panics. That is, they change the core interactions of the panic response sequence.

Review your practices over the preceding two weeks. Did you practice the various activities that you had outlined as producing sensations or heightening your awareness of sensations in a way that had previously frightened you? Did you practice each activity a sufficient number of times in order to feel in control of your emotional response while performing those activities? Did you practice your activities regularly as opposed to waiting until the last two days before returning to this book?

If you have not practiced regularly the activities that were previously outlined, or if you have not practiced all of the activities that you specified, then continue to do those practices before you proceed to the following material. It is essential that you maintain your focus upon achieving control of your emotional responses by prioritizing these practices. It takes effort, but the more effort you put out the more benefit you will gain. Remember to keep records of your practices as specified last time.

Did you have the experience of trying one of your activities, becoming frightened and escaping the situation? For example, did you sit in a sauna for a short period of time and leave as soon as you began to feel too hot. If that is the case, then spend some time now evaluating your response. What were the elements that resulted in your escape? What kind of physical sensations did you experience? What kind of self-statements were going through your mind and how did those two result in your escape? Try to understand why you did not return to the activity. What was the source of your hesitation to re-enter? Remember that avoidance of those activities serves to confirm your fear and your perception that you cannot cope. Control can only be obtained by overcoming that initially very strong urge to escape. That is, initially you may, indeed, feel a very strong wish to get out of the situation, but it is essential that you evaluate the basis for that urge to escape. Only by so doing will you then be able to understand that, although you may feel a very strong need to escape, you can in fact endure the activity.

Remember that these practices are not supposed to be associated with zero anxiety or fear. That is, you are expected to feel afraid initially, but with repeated practice, the fear level will decrease. If you did escape, then evaluate your response of escape and return to the activity from which you withdrew. Repeat your confrontation enough times until you feel comfortable while doing the activity. Then you can practice further by extending the intensity of the activity. For instance, if your practice was jogging for ten minutes, and you have done that enough times to feel comfortable, then jog for twenty minutes (if this is within your physical capabilities). If you feel that you have accomplished the activities in the way specified, then continue with the following material in this chapter.

Conquering Agoraphobia - Back to the Shopping Mall

In the first chapter we talked about phobia or the tendency to avoid places or situations because of fear or panic when no real danger exists. People with panic attacks often avoid, at least to some degree, places or situations where escape might be difficult in the event of a panic attack. The shopping mall is the typical example but a list of typical places or situations avoided is presented in Table 13:1. This avoidance is called agoraphobic avoidance and it can last even after you have mastered your panic attacks. Therefore, just as with the activities that you have practiced, there may be several or more situations that you have avoided, escaped from or endured with intense levels of fear or panic. These situations may, in themselves, not necessarily directly produce physical sensations (unlike physical exercise and other activities we discussed in the last chapter) but produce a feeling of panic and anxiety and the associated physical symptoms because you anticipate panicking in those situations.

The first step is to develop a list of situations that you typically fear and avoid. Place them in order of difficulty from the least difficult to the most difficult situation. As with the activities, the best method of changing your reactions to those situations is by confronting those situations repeatedly in a controlled manner. To increase the benefit of that confrontation, we will include the additional techniques of (1) imaginally rehearsing before actually confronting the situation and (2) attempting to experience deliberately the physical sensations that have been associated with panic while in those situations. You may find that when you confront the different situations you have

Table 13:1

<u>Typical Agoraphobic - Avoided Situations</u>

Shopping malls
Driving
Car passenger
Bus passenger
Trains
Subways
Wide streets
Tunnels
Restaurants
Theatres
Being a long way
from home
Staying at home alone
Waiting in lines
Supermarkets
Stores
Crowds
Planes
Elevators
Escalators

avoided in the past, you experience very little anxiety. However, it is important that the absence of anxiety is not due solely to the absence of particular sensations when you are in that situation. To benefit most, it is essential that you can experience panic-related physical symptoms, such as dizziness or palpitations, while you are in a shopping mall or while you are driving a car without becoming frightened. Therefore, when you make your hierarchy of different situations, base your rank order of difficulty on the assumption that in each situation you would also experience the sensations that have frightened you.

Try to specify as clearly as possible the aspects of the situation which distress you. For example, driving on a road may not be sufficient as, for you, it might be driving on particular roads that is most frightening. Similarly, shopping in a grocery store may not be specific enough because it may depend on the time of day, whether you are alone or with someone else, whether the store is crowded or not, etc. Specify the aspects that disturb you most. That is essential because the practices must be designed to fit the particular aspects of which you are most afraid. Otherwise, the purpose of the practice is lost. Again, practicing driving on a road may not be very helpful if you only practice on roads that don't typically frighten you. An example is given below of specific situations of which Jill was afraid.

Table 13:2

<u>Jill's Specification of Situation - Exposure Tasks</u>

Shopping in a crowded supermarket for 30 minutes alone.

Walking five blocks away from home alone.

Driving on a busy highway for five miles with husband, and alone.

Eating in a restaurant, seated in the middle.

Watching a movie while seated in the middle of the row.

Otherwise, the purpose of the practice is lost. Again, practicing driving on a road may not be very helpful if you only practice on roads that don't typically frighten you. An example is given below of specific situations of which Jill was afraid.

In terms of the way you approach these situations, extensive research suggests that a very effective method is to proceed gradually. That means starting with the items that are least distressing to you and gradually working up the list and breaking down each item from the list into different steps. You will recognize that this is the way we have approached every task. For example, if you have chosen to practice shopping for a half hour in a grocery store, it might be helpful to initially shop for 10 minutes and gradually build to 30 minutes. This is the approach we recommend particularly if you are doing this largely on your own.

On the other hand, the alternative approach is to take the bull by the horns, and start with the most difficult item. This means accepting that you will feel a lot of fear initially, and it requires a lot of motivation beforehand. However, the method is based on the same principles as described above, except the intensive procedure often produces results faster. This is a decision for you to make; either gradual or intense confrontation. Either way, a lot of planning beforehand is required, and it is essential that you follow through with your plan. At this point, it is helpful to have the supervision or prompting by another person, such as a family member and/or the professional with whom you're working.

Much of your daily life has probably entailed entering different situations that have frightened you, but obviously, it has not worked therapeutically in terms of reducing your fear. Otherwise, you would not be looking for this kind of treatment. That fact highlights the need to do this kind of practice in a very controlled and structured way.

Make your choice of method. Whether you have chosen the gradual or intense method, there are several steps through which to proceed. <u>First</u>, as a means of helping you to structure your practice and maintain your focus, it is helpful to imaginally rehearse the situation. Included in the imaginal rehearsal is your experience of intense physiological sensations and anxious, escapist-oriented self-

"It's the mailman, doc. He scares me."

statements. Also included in your imaginal rehearsal, is your application of strategies that control your initial emotion of fear and escape. These strategies would be relaxation, rebreathing or self-statement modification. That is, the imagination is not designed to be purely non-anxiety provoking. It is most effective to imagine yourself feeling very frightened and then to imagine yourself controlling that fear and staying in the situation. This will prepare you for the actual experience.

Second, and related to the first, is the importance of accepting and even exaggerating the physical sensations during the actual practice. The exposure is not as effective if you try to prevent feeling any physical sensations. If your first item is to enter a shopping mall, then say to yourself, before you enter the mall, that you expect to feel dizzy or lightheaded and you're going to try to make yourself feel dizzier or more lightheaded. This involves a very different approach to those sensations than before. Entering a situation with the intention of experiencing intense physical sensations is evidence of no longer being fearful of those sensations. If you have difficulty understanding the rationale, it would be worthwhile for you to reread some of the previous material in the earlier chapters. You should be at the point right now of really going for it.

For each practice, as you did with the practices with different activities, it is important to keep records of your progress, using the same EXPOSURE RECORD form. Practice each item the number of times that it is necessary for you to be able to enter the situation without feeling out of control. That is, repeat the practice the number of times necessary for your level of anxiety or fear to reach two. Again, spacing between practices of a particular situation, will depend largely on practical concerns. Driving may be easier to repeat in quick succession than staying home alone. However, if you do your repetitions within one "practice session" (e.g., one afternoon) attempt no more than three repetitions at any one time. If your fear level is still greater than two after three repetitions in one day, just start again the next day. It is important that you schedule your practices regularly. Do not wait - start today. The amount of practice and the number of situations practiced will differ from one person to another person. For that reason, a specific time interval is not recommended. However, it would be very helpful for you to reread this particular section of the book at least once every week in order to remind you of how to do the practices and continue your focus upon the practices. Do not stop your progress at this point. Keep working at it if you really want to reap the benefits.

It is often helpful to have the aid of a friend or family member when practicing going into different situations of which you are afraid. If you do have a helper, ensure that they have a clear understanding of the purpose of your practices, and that you give them a clear description of the nature of your anxiety and fear. Their presence is useful for two reasons.

(1) As a way of doing your practices more gradually, if that is the approach you have chosen. For example, if you have difficulty shopping in a crowded mall, it may be easier if you initially practice with someone. However, it is essential that you then continue to practice alone so that you learn that you are not in danger when alone.

(2) As a means of providing external prompts to apply the appropriate strategies. That is, your aide could remind you to use breathing or relaxation techniques whenever they notice breathing irregularity or tension. In addition, at regular intervals, your aide could remind you to evaluate and modify your self-statements.

For both reasons, it is very important that you and your aide are very clear on the role of each person. The last thing you want is to get into an argument because you feel pressured by your aide when you are in the shopping mall. Similarly, it would be defeating the purpose of having the aide if you become frustrated and angry when your aide tries to prompt your use of panic management strategies.

Exercise

Practice your confrontation with the different situations using either gradual or intensive methods with the structure that was specified and the help of an additional person if possible. Imaginally rehearse dealing with your anxiety/fear before each practice. Plan for regular practice of your different situations, keeping a record of your levels of anxiety/fear with each practice on the EXPOSURE RECORD form. Repeat your practice the number of times that is necessary for your level of fear/anxiety to reach two or less. Plan for the repetitions according to practical issues, but do not practice one situation more than three times in any one "session", even if the fear levels have not reduced to a level of two. Just start again the following day. Otherwise, you will simply exhaust yourself. Continue with these practices for the next two weeks or longer if you have not dealt with all the different situations. Reread this chapter at least once a week to keep youself focused on the program and the correct method of exposure practice.

Self-Assessment

Answer each of the following by circling true (T) or false (F). Answers are on page A-6.

1. It is essential that you do not even think about your feelings when you go into different situations.   T   F

2. You may practice confronting situations in either a gradual or an intense fashion, but the most important aspect is to do your practices in a very structured and controlled manner.   T   F

3. Practice each situation once only.   T   F

4. Experiencing anxiety or fear when you are in the situation means you have failed.   T   F

5. Practices must be done regularly.   T   F

CHAPTER 14

Medication Issues

Review

Review your DAILY MOOD and PANIC ATTACK RECORDS. Add the average daily anxiety and number of panic attacks per week to your PROGRESS RECORD. What changes can you see? What about your use of breathing retraining or relaxation techniques? Did you apply those strategies when you practiced entering different situations or at any time when you noticed physical symptoms or anxiety? Have you had any panic attacks that at first seemed to be unexpected? What precipitants could you find? Have you continued to correct overestimations and decatastrophize? What about your ratings on your SELF-STATEMENT RATING FORM? Are you becoming more confident in your ability to cope and/or less expectant of negative things happening?

Now, what about your practice in different situations? Did you practice regularly? If not, then continue with those practices before proceeding to the following material. Otherwise, you are defeating the purpose of this whole program, to overcome your fear. Go through your list of situations that you avoid, or enter with a lot of fear and hesitation, and rank them again in order of difficulty. Plan for your practices - when and how you will do each one. Imaginally rehearse managing your anxiety/fear. Using either the gradual or intense method, repeat your practices the number of times necessary for you to feel no more than mild levels of distress. Remember you can use the aid of a family member or friend to help you with gradual practicing (first accompanied and then alone) and to prompt your use of appropriate strategies of breathing retraining, or relaxation, and modification of self-statements. Also, remember to go in with the approach of experiencing physical symptoms to the fullest. Do not try to avoid the feeling of dizziness, or a racing heart, and so on. Also, try not to deliberately distract yourself while you are practicing, but focus on where you are and how you feel in a very objective manner. If you have practiced all of your situations (or most of them) and you feel comfortable in each one, continue with the following material.

If you're like many people with anxiety and panic attacks you have probably already been to see your family physician who has prescribed a minor tranquilizer for your anxiety. You may be taking this medication regularly or perhaps only occasionally when you feel you need it, for example when you feel particularly anxious. Many people go through this program without ever starting medication; others would just as soon not take the medication but are doing so on the advice of their physicians. However, there are a number of people who desire medication for their anxiety and/or panic attacks for a variety of reasons. For some, the anxiety and panic are so overwhelmingly severe that they feel they cannot tolerate even one more day and desire relief just as soon as possible. Even the drug that takes the longest period of time to act would begin to take effect in three weeks. Some of the shorter acting drugs can be effective within a day or two. There is no question that those effects are quicker than one is likely to experience while going through the lessons in this program unless one is able to devote a great deal of time to it and work through the lessons very quickly. Others may not feel that they have the time to devote to mastering the information in this workbook at the present time. Still others may believe strongly that medication is the most appropriate treatment for their anxiety.

In any case, as we mentioned in the first chapter, almost 75% of the people who come to our clinic for treatment are taking some kind of medication for their anxiety. Naturally, some of the people coming to our clinic who are on medication are still suffering from their anxiety and panic or they wouldn't bother to come. For others, their family physician has given them a prescription to get them through the next couple of weeks but told them to come to our clinic as soon as possible.

As we mentioned in the first chapter, we do not recommend that these people stop taking their drugs before starting the program. Eventually many people stop on their own. Approximately half of the people completing this program stop taking drugs on their own (usually with the consent of their physician) by the time they finish this program, and others stop sometime during the first year after they finish the program. We will describe below methods for using this program to help you stop taking drugs if you want to.

At this point the evidence seems quite clear that several classes of drugs, if prescribed at the appropriate dosage, would be effective for at least the short-term relief of anxiety or panic for some people. Many of these drugs, however, are not effective in the long term unless you continue to take them indefinitely. Even then, they may lose some of their effectiveness unless you learn some new, more adaptive methods of coping with your anxiety and panic while you are on the drug. There are also some individuals who begin a course of drug therapy and stop several months later without any need to go through a program such as this. Whether the particular stress they were under has resolved itself or whether there were some neurobiological changes in their "sensitivity" or whether they developed a different attitude towards their anxiety and panic, this is the only treatment they needed.

For all of these reasons it seems useful to review briefly the types of medications prescribed for anxiety and panic and indications for their use based on current knowledge.

Benzodiazepines (Minor Tranquilizers)

By far the drugs most commonly prescribed for anxiety and panic are the minor tranquilizers. Types and brand names of minor tranquilizers are far too numerous to mention here, but two of the most commonly prescribed medications are diazepam (Valium) and chlordiazepoxide (Librium).

Typically these drugs are prescribed for short-term relief of anxiety but are generally believed to be ineffective for panic attacks unless they are prescribed in very high dosages with which your family physician may not feel comfortable. For example, you might need 30 mg. or more of Valium a day to make a dent in your panic attacks. And yet, at this dosage, chances are you would feel very sedated. For this reason, minor tranquilizers are very seldom prescribed for panic attacks by psychiatrists knowledgeable in the drug treatment of this problem. Additional well-known difficulties with minor tranquilizers involve a tendency to require a greater dosage of the drug to obtain the same anxiety reducing effect. Unless you work carefully with your physician, there is a danger that you may become psychologically and physically dependent on the drug which is intended only for short-term treatment of anxiety.

High Potency Benzodiazepines

One of the most interesting advances lately in drug treatment has been the discovery that high potency benzodiazepines, which do not have the sedative effects of the minor tranquilizers, seem effective in reducing panic attacks, at least in the short term. By far, the best known high potency benzodiazepine is alprazolam (Xanax), and clonazepam (clonopin) is also an increasingly prescribed treatment for panic disorder. To give you an idea of how strong Xanax is, 1 mg. of Xanax equals 10 mg. of Valium. The appropriate dosage of Xanax to deal with panic disorder, based on a recent important study by the Upjohn Company (makers of Xanax), is 6 to 10 mg. a day. Taking 10 mg. of Xanax would be taking the equivalent of 100 mg. of Valium.

While on these dosages, 60% of a large group of patients were free of panic after eight weeks of treatment with this drug. This is a very good result. However, it seems that one becomes very dependent on this drug since it is very difficult for a majority of people to stop taking it once they have started. This is because when one stops taking it one experiences either a quick reoccurrence of the anxiety or some withdrawal effects of the drug or probably a combination of both. These effects are very unpleasant. Approximately 30% of patients experience this anxiety and panic more intensely than they ever experienced it before starting treatment. For this reason, almost everyone relapses once taken off the drug, particularly if one is taken off too quickly. This drug must be tapered very slowly under the close supervision of a physician, preferably a psychiatrist.

Anti-depressants

There are two types of anti-depressants that seem effective for anxiety and panic attacks. The first type is the tricyclic anti-depressants such as imipramine (Tofranil) and amytriptyline (Elavil). Tofranil is by far the most commonly used antidepressant for anxiety and panic. Another type of anti-depressant drug is the monoamine-oxidase inhibitors (MAO inhibitors). The best known drug in this category for anxiety and panic is phenelzine (Nardil). All of these drugs seem approximately equal in effectiveness for panic attacks as well as agoraphobic avoidance, particularly when combined with the type of program presented in this manual. The major difficulty with these drugs is that during the first two or three weeks, one typically experiences a number of side effects that seem to some people to be very similar to anxiety. For that reason, many people do not want to continue taking the drug or at least do not want to increase the dosage to appropriate therapeutic levels. And yet, research has demonstrated that it is very important to take enough of this drug to get the full therapeutic benefits. For example, most people should be taking at least 150 mg. per day of Tofranil to get the maximum therapeutic benefit. Naturally, this will vary somewhat depending on your physician's judgment. Therefore, if at all possible one should persevere through the first several weeks of taking this drug until reaching that therapeutic dosage.

The MAO inhibitors are used less frequently for panic attacks because there are severe dietary restrictions with which one must comply when taking the drug. For example, one should not eat cheese, chocolate, or other foods containing tyramine nor drink red wine or beer. If you do, you risk a variety of dangerous symptoms including very high blood pressure. If you're comfortable with avoiding these foods, then you should be taking over 50 mg. a day of the most popular drug, Nardil, to get the full therapeutic benefit.

It is much easier to stop taking tricyclic anti-depressants than to terminate benzodiazepines whether high potency or not. Therefore, the relapse rates are much lower for anti-depressants, perhaps as low as 30%. The evidence suggests that anti-depressants are most effective when combined with a program such as contained in this manual.

Beta Blockers

Many people take beta blockers in order to reduce blood pressure or regulate heart rate. These drugs act on a specific receptor, the beta receptor, which is involved in physiological arousal. Therefore, if one needs to avoid physiological arousal for medical reasons, beta blockers are often prescribed. Again, there are a large number of beta blockers available, but the most popular remains propranolol (Inderal). One would think that any medication reducing physical sensations of which people might be frightened would have some effect. Nevertheless, there is very little if any evidence that Inderal is useful in any way for panic attacks and associated anxiety, although occasionally someone might feel a little bit better. For that reason, psychiatrists knowledgeable about the drug treatment of anxiety almost never prescribe this drug to treat anxiety and panic.

Stopping Your Drug Use

Now that you have completed this program, you should be ready to stop your medication if you so desire. Chances are you already have done so. If not, be very sure that you stop taking your medication under the supervision of your physician; only he or she can decide how quickly it will be safe for you to taper your medication to the point where you eliminate it altogether. This will be particularly true for drugs like Xanax which are very hard to stop taking. Nevertheless, with what you have learned from this program you should have little trouble stopping your medication if you follow these guidelines.

1. Withdraw from your medication relatively slowly. Don't try to do it all at once. Once again, your physician will be able to give you the best advice on what schedule of withdrawal is appropriate for you.

2. Set a target date for stopping your medication altogether. Once again, this will have to be planned with your physician so make it a reasonable date in view of your own tapering schedule. On the other hand, the date should not be too far away. Generally, the quicker the better as long as it is within a schedule that is reasonable for you as determined by your physician.

3. Use the principles and coping skills that you have learned in this manual as you withdraw from the medication.

The reason that we have not addressed this topic until now is because it's important for you to learn how to master your anxiety and panic before successfully eliminating your medication. One of the major reasons for this is that you may begin to experience anxiety and panic at somewhat more intense levels as you withdraw from medication. If you were never on medication, you should have mastered panic and anxiety in all of its manifestations by now. If you are on medication, the principles you have learned will need to be applied again to deal with some reemergence of anxiety and panic as you come off medication. Once again, most people do not find this a problem and gradually reduce their medication as they become more comfortable in dealing with their anxiety and panic. These people never experience a serious new outbreak of panic as they withdraw from their medication. However, if for some reason your anxiety and panic seems to be increasing, particularly if you were on one of the benzodiazepines, you should be reassured by the fact that this reemergence will only last a week or two at most until the drug clears from your system. In addition, you now have the skills to handle this anxiety and perhaps eliminate it entirely.

In fact, withdrawal from medication can be considered the last item or activity on your list of activities in your daily life described in Chapters 11 and 12 where you produced the panic sensations on your own. For some of you, withdrawing from medication is another excellent way to produce panic sensations. Therefore, this is an opportunity to apply your strategies for reducing fear and anxiety. Rather than becoming distressed at any sensation that you experience as you withdraw from drugs, you should follow the guidelines in Chapters 11 and 12 and accentuate these sensations through your exercises until any anxiety you experience is reduced. Of course, you can continue to use your breathing control or relaxation training along with your cognitive strategies such as analysis of causes and prediction testing during this period.

In other words, treat withdrawal from medication as an excellent final opportunity to develop total mastery over your emotions and disintegrate once and for all the terrifying sensations of panic. The rewards will be worth it.

Exercise

If you are on medication and wish to withdraw, then your assignment for this week is to speak with your prescribing physician about the best procedure for withdrawal. Also, plan how you will deal with any of the withdrawal effects by using the various strategies and exposure principles described throughout. Draw up a specific step-by-step plan for yourself.

Self-Assessment

Answer each of the following by circling true (T) or false (F). Answers are on page A-7.

1. It is essential that withdrawal from medication
   is conducted gradually, under the supervision
   of your prescribing physician.   T   F

2. You are unlikely to feel any different when you withdraw
   from your medication.   T   F

3. Use any symptoms and anxiety or panic that you experience
   when withdrawing from medication as an opportunity to
   apply relaxation/breathing control, self-statement
   strategies and exposure principles.   T   F

4. Experiencing physical symptoms or anxiety/panic when
   withdrawing from medication is a sign of loss of
   all your treatment gains.   T   F

CHAPTER 15

Your Accomplishments and Your Future

Several important issues need to be addressed in this final chapter:

1. Examine the changes that you have experienced since you first began this program.

2. Determine what is the next step.

3. Consider methods of maintaining the progress that you have achieved.

4. Consider high-risk situations for the future and how to deal with your reactions and strategies to implement.

Self-Evaluation

It is time to consider the kind of changes that you have made since you first began this program. This can be done in several ways. A very objective method is to examine the DAILY ANXIETY and PANIC ATTACK RECORDS that you have been keeping of the frequency and intensity of your experiences of panic and anxiety. Using your PROGRESS RECORD, examine the changes from the beginning until now. First, compare the frequency from the beginning to this point and examine the course of change throughout the program. There may, indeed, be ups and downs. If you have experienced what you consider to be a significant reduction in the frequency and/or intensity of your episodes of panic and anxiety, check yes in the box next to the item labeled panic and anxiety in the list below.

Second, look at your SELF-STATEMENT RATING form. Examine the changes in your evidence-based estimates of the probability and your ability to cope with your most distressing events in your panic experiences and/or your anxiety experiences. If you consider that you have experienced a significant reduction in your estimate of the probability and significant increases in your perceived ability to cope with either or both of those experiences, check the yes box item labeled self-statements.

Third, look at your initial record of ratings of fear in response to the symptom induction exercises (in Chapter 10). Now, next to those items rate your current level, using the 0 to 8 point scale. If there has been a significant reduction in the fear you associate with the majority of items from that list of exercises, indicate yes below in the box next to the item labeled symptom exercises.

Fourth, take the list of activities that you identified as initially being associated with fear and/or avoidance because of the sensations they produced. Now go back and rate your level of fear of each activity and also rate your level of avoidance of each activity using the 0 to 8 point scale (where 0 = no fear/avoidance and 8 = extreme fear/avoidance). If you experienced a significant reduction in your fear and avoidance of those activities, check the yes box next to the item labeled activities.

Table 15:1

<u>Self Evaluation</u>

<u>Panic and Anxiety</u>
Significant reduction in frequency and/or intensity of panic
and anxiety episodes.

☐ ☐
YES NO

<u>Self-Statements</u>
Significant reduction in estimates of probability and/or
increase in perceived ability to cope with most distressing
events.

☐ ☐
YES NO

<u>Symptom Exercises</u>
Significant reduction in fear of symptom induction exercises.

☐ ☐
YES NO

<u>Activities</u>
Significant reduction in fear and/or avoidance of activities
associated with panic symptoms.

☐ ☐
YES NO

<u>Situations</u>
Significant reduction in fear and/or avoidance of situations.

☐ ☐
YES NO

Fifth, go back to your initial list of <u>agoraphobic situations</u> that you feared and avoided. Rate each one as you currently feel in terms of level of fear and level of avoidance on 0 to 8 point scales. If you've experienced a significant reduction in your fear and avoidance of those situations, check the <u>yes</u> box next to the item labeled situations.

If you have checked the <u>yes</u> box for at least three of those five items, you may consider that you have done very well with this program. If, on the other hand, you have checked <u>no</u> to three or more items, it suggests that there is still room for gains to be made.

<u>What To Do Next</u>

On the basis of the point system established above, decide whether you have responded well to the program or you are someone who has room for much more benefit. If you fit into the former category, then your strategy should be to identify any areas where you still have concerns and to continue in the same way as you have done throughout the program. Identify concerns that remain in either your understanding of panic, avoidance of activities or situations, or response to physical sensations and apply the strategies that you have learned. Review different sections of the book to help you to deal with areas of remaining difficulty.

If you decide that there is still a lot of room for change, then it is important at this point to try to evaluate possible reasons for that result. There are several possible reasons:

1.   The initial series of decisions concerning the appropriateness of this program may not have been accurate, in which case discussion with your doctor or mental health professional should center upon further assessment.

2.   The program simply requires a longer time for some individuals depending on various factors. That is not necessarily an indication of the lack of success of the program but simply an indication of the need for continued application of the strategies as described. If so, continue in the way that you have begun, under the assumption that there has been some change from the beginning of the program until now. If no progress has occurred, then the first possibility listed above may be more accurate.

3.   The program is appropriate but the amount of effort you have put in has not been sufficient. This is the most common reason. Have you practiced regularly and sufficiently? This might include examples where crises (such as marital discord) have occurred during the course of your involvement in the program that have taken your attention away. If so, the success of the program simply depends on renewed effort and motivation. If motivation is a more general issue then it may be better to leave the program aside until a future time when you're feeling more motivated.

4.   The fourth possibility is that you have not fully integrated the major principles of the program, such as the definition of panic. If this is the case, then a review of all the principles preferably with your doctor or mental health professional is warranted.

Maintenance Planning

If you have done well with this program or are still in the process of achieving control by continued application of the principles from this program, then one issue to keep in mind is the maintenance of your results. Sometimes people ask, "will I always be anxious", and "does the application of these strategies simply mean that I'm suppressing an underlying anxiety that is always going to be there". In response to the first question, it is important to note that anxiety is a perfectly normal human trait; all of us experience anxiety and, in fact, it would be unadaptive to remove anxiety from our lives because it plays such a big role in motivation for performance. We talked about this in the first chapter. Learning to control excessive levels of anxiety is like any other learned behavior; once it is learned it is most likely that under the usual and customary conditions, it will become more powerful with time and, therefore, more resistant to change. There are certain factors which may relate to the likelihood of experiencing at some time in the future an increase in your level of anxiety, and those high risk times will be discussed below.

In response to the second question, it is important to note that this program is not intended as a way of suppressing underlying anxiety. Rather, the methods that you have been taught are intended as a means of changing the quality of your experiences so that you no longer experience excessive anxiety or fear. You are learning to reach the core of your anxiety and fear reactions and change them. The emotion is always going to be present because, as mentioned before, anxiety is a very natural human quality, but what you have learned up to this point is to control the unadaptive expression of that emotion. You have learned this control in response to certain elements, such as sensations, activities or situations that are not inherently dangerous and, therefore, do not inherently warrant that emotion. In other words, you have gained control of your emotion.

There are certain key factors that promote the continuation of the accomplishments you have made during the program. They are as follows. First, whenever you notice yourself hesitating to enter the types of situations or to perform the types of activities described throughout this manual for reasons of fear, that should be an indication to you to go ahead and do it. Do not allow your emotions to direct your behavior. Second, make a point of trying to experience all of the sensations that have been associated with your panic in the past to the fullest. In other words, do things that bring on the sensations and continuously reinforce your newly developed sense of control. Third, whenever you do experience anxiety or fear, remember to use the objective scientific analysis that we have developed in the preceding chapters. Rather than being overwhelmed by your fear reactions, evaluate the precipitants, evaluate the sequencing or the interactions that occurred, and understand very clearly how the emotion arose. Only in cases where there is a real danger, such as an on-coming car that is heading directly for you, being robbed or mugged or confronting a clearly vicious dog, should your fear be considered a rational element that need not be questioned.

In general, it might be helpful at times to review some of the material in these chapters by re-reading different sections. If you do experience fear at some time in the future that seems initially to be a "panic attack" or initially frightens you, first, do not treat that as a relapse and a sense that you have lost everything that you have gained. That is a time when you must apply, to the fullest extent, an approach of objective understanding. Try to analyze for yourself the reasons for which the fear occurred and re-apply some of the same strategies that have been described previously. Indeed, you may expect that at some time in the future, you will become frightened again. Try not to allow yourself to get into the avoidant responding of always hoping that you will never feel that way again. If that is something that you say to yourself, then it is an indication that you have not learned to understand fear differently.

High Risk Times

From our work, it has been established that the likelihood of becoming fearful again is increased at times when you experience a lot of stress in your life, including both positive and negative stress, physical illness, loss of a significant other and so on. It seems that the stress affects your central nervous system in a way that makes you generally more physiologically aroused or tense as we described in earlier chapters. Consequently, you are more likely to experience different kinds of sensations. The important thing to realize is that if you do become frightened by the sensations, there are probably some unadaptive interactions going on between your interpretations and your feelings. That is, experiencing stress and the physiological effects of stress does not equal anxiety and panic.

Anxiety and panic only develop when you respond to that stress and physiological activation unadaptively. That response is under your control.

Finally, <u>congratulations</u> on finishing this program! You've worked very hard to get to this point and you deserve all of the credit in the world for the work that you've done. We sincerely hope that you're well on your way to regaining control over your life and that you've escaped from the grasp of your negative emotions. Perhaps you're there already. If so, then we hope that you're under the influence of another emotion - you can feel this one in the form of satisfaction with your success.

ANSWERS FOR SELF-ASSESSMENT QUESTIONS

CHAPTER 2

1. True. Monitoring is an essential component to the development of control over anxiety and fear as it provides the basis from which to understand your emotions and implement appropriate strategies.

2. False. Avoiding thinking about your feelings is understandable when the feelings are distressing but avoidance does not allow one to learn the core elements of different emotional reactions, which is a necessary ingredient for learning to control such reactions.

3. False. It is most effective to monitor panic attacks as soon as possible after their occurrence since recall tends to be biased and inaccurate.

4. True. Using monitoring techniques, one is able to determine the situations in which panic occurs most often and the factors which are most likely to precipitate panic. Identification of those factors is important to the development of a sense of control, as it heightens awareness of the fact that panic and anxiety are reactions rather than uncontrollable events.

5. True. Your levels of anxiety and depression and anticipation of panic can be recorded at the end of the day, by taking an overview of the day and calculating averages.

CHAPTER 3

1. True. The basic components to anxiety and fear are physiology, thoughts and behaviors, and it is the interaction among those three components which determines the intensity of the emotional responses of anxiety and fear.

2. False. Anxiety is a natural human emotion which everyone experiences and is indeed often a productive driving force. The goal of this program is to reduce levels of anxiety that are excessive and pervasive.

3. True. It is essential that you understand the interactions among physical sensations, interpretations and behaviors. By definition, panic includes physiological arousal and subjective fear. Hence, if there was no fear of the sensations, there would be no panic.

4. False. Hereditary factors seem to play some role in determining level of general sensitivity which may predispose some individuals to the development of anxiety, but hereditary does not explain all of panic.

5. True. Anxiety and panic are different emotions. The hallmark of panic is a sudden rush of fear with focus upon the immediate present, whereas anxiety is usually anticipatory in nature.

CHAPTER 4

1. False. While medical factors may be involved in panic attacks, a panic attack is not solely a medical problem over which you have no control. Panic is a reaction of fear to something, whether that something be a belief of being in danger or intense physiological arousal.

2. False. The symptoms experienced during panic, such as a racing heart and sweating, are natural sensations associated with arousal of the autonomic nervous system that occurs during episodes of fear. The physical symptoms reflect activation of a biological mechanism, which is, in fact, designed for the protection of the organism.

3. True. Panic is a fight or flight reaction designed to protect the organism against danger. In panic disorder, panic attacks occur in the absence of real danger.

4. True. While panics may seem unpredictable, they can always be tied to a cue or signal. Sometimes those cues are very subtle, such as fluctuations in breathing rate or intense emotion unrelated to fear, and, therefore, it seems as if the experience of panic is unpredictable.

5. False. The body's central nervous system has a built in inhibitor which counteracts activation of the sympathetic nervous system. Anticipatory anxiety may produce symptoms over long periods of time, but the actual panic attack is a relatively short event.

6. True. Going crazy is not a consequence of panicking. The worst that can happen during a panic attack is intense distress.

CHAPTER 5

1. a. True. Overbreathing refers to excessive inhalation of oxygen and a proportionate reduction in the level of carbon dioxide in the blood. If the body uses up oxygen at the rate at which it is inhaled, a state of overbreathing would not occur.

1. b. False. Continuous overbreathing may result in fainting. Fainting is an adaptive bodily response, during which time a balance between oxygen and carbon dioxide in the blood is reestablished.

1. c. False. During breathing retraining exercises, it is important to focus upon counting and the word "relax." The attention component to the exercise is important for learning to control patterns of fear and anxiety.

1. d. False. Speeding up of the breathing rate during breathing retraining exercises is an indication of the need to continue to practice and is probably a result of fearful hypersensitivity to breathing symptoms.

1. e. True. Breathing retraining is used as a technique to eliminate the symptoms which have become signals for panicking and to reduce the level of physiological arousal that occurs during panic attacks.

2. a. False. Physical tension can occur both acutely and chronically, but the long-term presence of tension does not imply an inability to achieve relaxed states.

2. b. True. Experiencing excessive levels of muscular tension can exacerbate subjective feelings of anxious anticipation and fear.

2. c. True. A high level of muscular tension can produce fatigue, muscle aches, pains and weakness because of the excessive amount of energy used.

2. d. False. Learning to relax is achieved through progressive steps, the first of which is learning to relax the body very gradually by focusing on different muscle groups.

2. e. True. Relaxation methods are designed to eliminate the symptoms which have become cues to which the person is hypersensitive, and to reduce the level of physical tension which occurs during panic.

CHAPTER 6

1. True. Skipping out on practices once in a while is okay, but it is essential that, overall, practices be conducted regularly, and the amount of effort that is put into practicing determines the amount of benefit that is gained.

2. True. Focusing upon the techniques of breathing retraining and/or relaxation is essential to the effectiveness of these procedures. Learning to control emotional reactions entails a shifting of focus of attention away from sensations and feelings of being out of control to methods of being in control.

3. False. Just because it takes time to attain benefit from breathing retraining and/or relaxation, is not an indication that those techniques will never work.

4. True. Monitoring of exercises using relaxation and/or breathing retraining is very important for several reasons, including an awareness of their effectiveness and understanding reasons for which they were implemented more or less successfully.

CHAPTER 7

1. False. Thoughts impact greatly upon one's feelings just as one's feelings impact greatly upon thoughts. Thinking that danger is imminent will, of course, increase levels of anxiety and feeling anxious will increase the likelihood of thinking that one is in danger.

2. True. The first step in learning to correct anxiety provoking thoughts or self-statements that are inaccurate is to identify the thoughts or self statements as clearly and specifically as possible. Only then is one in a position to apply appropriate control techniques of questioning the evidence and decatastrophizing.

3.   False. The belief that self-statement modification is not effective because "I am still afraid that it could happen" is a contradiction in terms. Stating that you are afraid "it could still happen" indicates that the initial thought concerning danger or threat has not been modified.

4.   True. Questioning of one's thoughts enables one to interrupt the emotional cycle and examine the interactions between one's thoughts and feelings.

CHAPTER 8

1.   False. It is easy to confuse the presence of thoughts as an indication of their validity, but simply worrying about events such as fainting or going crazy does not increase the chance of those events actually happening.

2.   False. Everyone experiences unpleasant or distressing thoughts, but people differ in the frequency with which those thoughts occur.

3.   True. Despite feeling that it is hard to think rationally at times when you are very anxious or panicky, it is important to continue to evaluate what is going on in an objective manner. Use key questions such as "what am I worried about", "what are the real odds of that happening", "so what if it does happen", etc. Remember, even if you have difficulty thinking rationally, you will not be in any danger as the emotional state is transient and will pass.

4.   True. Forcing yourself to contemplate your worst fears will initially induce more anxiety but the most effective method of learning control is to face those concerns front on and to learn that they are invalid or inaccurate. By avoiding thinking about the things that frighten you, you are in some ways adding confirmatory evidence to those fearful images or thoughts.

CHAPTER 9

1.   True. While panic attacks may seem to occur unexpectedly, that is not an indication that the panics occur without reason and are, therefore, uncontrollable. In contrast, panic attacks are reactions, but sometimes the cues which stimulate the onset of panic are very subtle and hard to identify. In those cases, it might seem that the panic is unpredictable.

2.   False. Because a panic attack is seemingly unpredictable or "appears to come from out of the blue", it does not mean that the panic is more threatening. You are in no more danger when you experience a panic as a result of a specific event, such as giving a speech, than when you experience a panic while at home alone.

3.   False. While the methods of relaxation and/or breathing retraining are designed to control somatic symptoms, failure in applying those techniques will not result in increasing the chance of danger. They are simply management techniques, and even if you are not able to apply those techniques successfully, you would still survive panic.

4. True. Panic can be precipitated by a variety of events ranging from external, stressful happenings to subtle, internal events, such as a fluctuation in your heart rate or worrying about future panic attacks or feeling out of breath from running up a flight of stairs.

CHAPTER 10

1. True. An essential component to the therapy procedure is to allow yourself to experience the elements of which you are afraid to the fullest degree. That means experiencing the physical sensations at a very intense level and experiencing the feelings of anxiety fully. Failing to do so might result in a tendency to disconfirm the practices that you have done, and continue to fear that you would not be able to cope when the sensations or the anxiety do become intense.

2. False. Despite the general labels of panic disorder or anxiety disorder, there are many individual differences in the way in which anxiety and panic are experienced and the elements to which individuals are most sensitive. For that reason, you must tailor your practices to the elements of which you are most afraid.

3. True. Each exercise should be practiced repeatedly until the initial level of anxiety that is experienced is only mild. Remember that when you first begin to practice, you should not prevent the experience of anxiety: it is expected that initial anxiety/fear will be high and then will reduce with repeated practice.

4. False. Do not prevent the development of anxiety or fear before the exercise. That is, only use the management techniques of thought analysis or breathing retraining or relaxation after you have gone through the exercises.

CHAPTER 11

1. False. Re-experiencing panic after a period of time without panic is not an indication of relapse or loss of gains made. It simply reflects the need to continue to practice. It is very natural for people to re-experience panics at different times and, in fact, the experience of intense fear is a great opportunity for learning.

2. True. At times when the anxiety or fear are intense, it is helpful to identify the most feared event and ask a set of key questions such as "what are the real odds of this happening", and "so what if it does happen."

3. False. It is important to realize that by attempting to "fight off the feeling of fear at all costs" you are, in fact, not evaluating the reasons for experiencing fear and, therefore, not implementing appropriate methods of control. In addition, fighting off anxiety or fear adds fuel to the experience of anxiety or fear since fighting increases tension.

4. True. There is no question that the more practice you perform the more benefit you will gain. This point cannot be emphasized too much.

CHAPTER 12

1. False. If you become anxious or fearful when recalling your worst panic attacks, that is an indication of the need to continue to think about those past events until you are able to evaluate them objectively and to be less fearful of the memory. By avoiding thinking about those past events, you are maintaining a fear of their recurrence.

2. True. Daily practice is the most effective method of learning to change one's reactions, and the number of repetitions for each activity is dependent upon the level of anxiety experienced. Continue the activity the number of times required before you experience no more than mild levels of anxiety. However, do not practice more than five times in any one session because you will simply exhaust yourself.

3. True. The persistence of symptoms over a long period of time does not necessarily indicate that they are dangerous. It is likely that their persistence is based, at least in part, on your continuing attention to those symptoms and worry about them. By anxiously worrying about one's bodily symptoms, general levels of arousal are increased, and the presence of the symptoms is more likely.

4. True. It is important that the practices you conduct are carried out in a systematic and controlled manner. Begin with items that are low on your hierarchy and work up the hierarchy in a systematic manner.

CHAPTER 13

1. False. When practicing entering different situations that, in the past, you have avoided or have endured with anxiety/fear, it is important that you not only remain focused on where you are but also on what you feel in those situations. Trying to avoid the way that you feel may, in fact, alleviate the level of anxiety/fear at that moment but does not enable you to learn how to feel differently in the long term.

2. True. You can confront the situations which you have been avoiding or enduring with dread by using either a very intense approach or by a very gradual approach. Whatever approach you choose, the most important aspect is to do the practices regularly, systematically, and in a controlled manner. Use your self-monitoring to keep on track.

3. False. The number of practices that you conduct for each situation listed on your hierarchy is dependent on the level of anxiety that you experience. Continue to practice the number of times that is necessary in order to reduce your anxiety to a mild level.

4. False. You are, in fact, expected to experience some anxiety or fear when you first practice the situations that you have been avoiding or enduring with dread. The presence of anxiety or fear during your practice is certainly not an indication of failure, but an indication that you are facing the most relevant situations.

5. True. Practices must be done regularly.

CHAPTER 14

1. True. It is important that you do not withdraw from medication suddenly, and that you do not attempt to do this on your own.

2. False. It is likely that when you withdraw from medication you may experience physical symptoms that were controlled by the medication or anxiety related to the psychological dependence upon the medication. However, experiencing such symptoms or feelings is another opportunity for you to practice the different techniques that you have learned throughout this program.

3. True. Use the symptoms of anxiety and panic that you may experience when withdrawing from medication as an opportunity to apply relaxation/breathing control, self statement strategies, and exposure principles.

4. False. Experiencing the different symptoms when you withdraw from medication is not a sign of loss of your treatment gains, but is a very natural result of withdrawal.

CENTER FOR STRESS AND ANXIETY DISORDERS

The Center for Stress and Anxiety Disorders, under the direction of Drs. David H. Barlow and Edward B. Blanchard, is an internationally known clinical research center. The fundamental goal of the center is to develop new assessment and treatment procedures for the major anxiety and stress disorders that are so common in this country and around the world. To this end, some 500 new patients are evaluated each year with a majority benefiting from administration of the latest treatment developments. To support this effort the National Institutes of Health and the National Institute of Mental Health fund ongoing projects investigating new treatments for a variety of anxiety and stress disorders at a level approaching two million dollars per year. This makes the center the largest research clinic of its kind in the world.

ANXIETY DISORDERS INTERVIEW SCHEDULES

Revised ADIS (ADIS-R)

ISBN 1-880659-03-4

The purpose of this interview is to allow mental health and health professionals to make accurate and reliable diagnoses of people presenting with emotional disorders where anxiety is a prominent component. The format and specific wording of the questions, worked out over a period of eight years, is now fully compatible with DSM-III-R in this revised version and allows the clinician to ascertain the type and number of various anxiety and depressive disorders taking into account complications presented by other AXIS I disorders.

SPECIMEN SET is available (1 instruction manual and 1 ADIS-R; 60 pages saddle stitched, including summary score sheet). ISBN 1-880659-02-6

ADIS - P	ADIS - C
Parent Version	**Child Version**
ISBN 1-880659-06-9	**ISBN 1-880659-07-7**

Now available, our structured interview for the diagnosis of children presenting with emotional disorders, where anxiety is a prominent component. Developed and tested over the last 5 years by Dr. Wendy Silverman and the staff at the center, the interview yields a wealth of information concerning emotional disorders in children, particularly when accompanied by the companion interview for parents.

SPECIMEN SET is available (1 instruction manual and 1 ADIS-P and 1 ADIS-C; 39 pages, saddle stitched, including summary score sheets). ISBN 1-880659-05-0

THERAPIST'S GUIDE
(for MAP)
ISBN 1-880659-01-8

The Therapist's Guide for the Mastery of your Anxiety and Panic (MAP) program is designed to assist the clinician in facilitating therapeutic sessions structured around the MAP program. The conceptual basis for the treatment approach is provided, along with a rationale specific to each treatment procedure. An appreciation of the underlying principles allows the clinician to tailor the procedure to individual clients. Common pitfalls as well as typical and atypical reactions to various therapeutic procedures are also illustrated and solutions provided. For further information on theory, research and treatment of anxiety and related disorders, please see Barlow, D.H. Anxiety and Its Disorders: The Nature and Treatment of Anxiety and Panic. New York: Guilford Press (Guilford Publications, Inc., 72 Spring Street, New York, NY 10012-9941), 1988.

MAP - MONITORING FORMS - MAW
for Client Use

Many clients and therapists have requested separate packets of monitoring forms for the MAP and MAW programs. We are now pleased to provide all necessary forms for monitoring anxiety and panic symptoms as well as monitoring specific tasks assigned in the course of the program. These forms are packaged in a convenient manner such that one packet will be sufficient for one person to complete the whole program.

Clients in our setting have found particularly useful and convenient the panic attack records (daily worry records) provided in a 3 inch by 5 inch packet easily fitting pocket or purse. Clients fill in the one form each time they have a panic attack (attack of worry) and tear off the completed form from the packet for safe keeping.

CLINICIANS: Below is an order form should you care to have a client personally obtain the following materials. May we suggest, however, that you order the materials in bulk so that you have instant availability for your client. A form for your use is on the next page.

ORDER FORM
FOR
CLIENT USE

NAME _____

ADDRESS _____

_____

_____

PHONE _____

Number of MAPS requested _____ at $19.00 = _____

Number of Monitoring forms (MAP) _____ at $8.95 = _____

Number of MAWS requested _____ at $19.95 = _____

Number of Monitoring forms (MAW) _____ at $8.95 = _____

Shipping (4th cl) for U.S. residents: $2.00 per item = _____
Shipping (surface) for Canada and Foreign: $3.00 per item = _____
SUBTOTAL= _____
* NY Residents: Add appropriate sales tax to subtotal = _____
TOTAL = _____

* As of 10/1/91 all NY orders must include sales tax calculated on the cost of the item as well as on the shipping and handling fees.

Please remit ALL orders in <u>U.S. $.</u> Pre-payment in U.S funds is required on all overseas shipments. All orders that do not include shipping and handling fees or applicable taxes will be returned.

Make checks payable and mail to:

GRAYWIND PUBLICATIONS
c/o 1535 Western Avenue
Albany, New York 12203

Allow 3-4 weeks for delivery
Allow 6-8 weeks for delivery outside of North America

ORDER FORM
FOR
CLINICIAN

TITLE	QUANTITY	PRICE	TOTAL
Mastery of Your Anxiety and Panic (MAP)		See Rate Chart	
Therapist's Guide for the MAP		$25.00	
MAP Monitoring Forms for Client Use		See Rate Chart	
Mastery of Your Anxiety and Worry (MAW)		See Rate Chart	
MAW Monitoring Forms for Client Use		See Rate Chart	
ADIS-R Specimen Set (1 instruction manual & 1 ADIS-R)		$11.50	
ADIS-R (MINIMUM set of 10 required)		See Rate Chart	
ADIS-P & C Specimen Set (1 set of instructions & 1 ADIS-P & 1 ADIS-C)		$14.50	
ADIS-P & C (MINIMUM set of 10 required)		See Rate Chart	

Shipping Charges   (see rate chart)

SUBTOTAL   =

*N.Y. Residents ADD appropriate sales tax to subtotal

TOTAL (U.S. $) =

BULK RATES FOR MAP	
Number of Copies	Cost Per Copy
1-10 ....$19.00	
11-20 ....$18.50	
21-50 ....$17.75	
51+ $17.00	

BULK RATES FOR MAW	
Number of Copies	Cost Per Copy
1-10 ....$19.95	
11-20 ....$19.45	
21-50 ....$18.70	
51+ $17.95	

Shipping Charges		
Number of Copies	U.S. Rate	Canadian & Foreign
1-2	$3.00	$4.00
3-10	7% of Subtotal	15% of Subtotal
11-20	6% of Subtotal	14% of Subtotal
21-50	5% of Subtotal	13% of Subtotal
51 and Over	4% of Subtotal	12% of Subtotal

BULK RATES FOR ADIS		
ADIS-R	ADIS-P	ADIS-C
MINIMUM set of 10 (e.g. 10 ADIS-R's OR 5 ADIS-P's + 5 ADIS-C's)		
10 ....$4.00 per schedule		
50 or more ....$3.75 per schedule		
100 or more ....$3.50 per schedule		

See ordering information on the reverse side

MAP	BULK RATES FOR MONITORING FORMS	MAW
Number of Packets		**Cost Per Packet**
1-25		$8.95
26-49		$8.75
50 or more		$8.50

All orders that do not include shipping and handling fees or applicable taxes will be returned. For faster service, you may fax an authorized purchase order and/or your over night mailing account number with your pre-payment. We will process your order within 3 working days.

Pre-payment in U.S. funds is required on all overseas shipments.

Remit all payments in U.S. $
Make check payable & mail to:

GRAYWIND PUBLICATIONS
c/o 1535 Western Avenue
Albany, New York 12203

Allow 3-4 weeks for delivery
Allow 6-8 weeks for delivery outside of the U.S.

Please Print Clearly:

NAME _____

ADDRESS _____

_____

PHONE _____